W9-BSU-327

(continued)

Critical Literacy in the Early Childhood Classroom

Unpacking Histories, Unlearning Privilege

Candace R. Kuby

Foreword by Vivian M. Vasquez

Teachers College, Columbia University
New York and London

Published by Teachers College Press, 1234 Amsterdam Avenue, New York 10027

Grateful acknowledgment is made for the following:

Chapter 1 excerpts from Kuby, C.R., 2012. Personal histories and pedagogical decisions: Using autoethnographic methods to unpack ideologies and experiences. *Teaching & Learning: The Journal of Natural Inquiry and Reflective Practice*. Reprinted with permission.

Chapter 3 excerpts from Kuby, C. R., 2011. Kidwatching with a critical eye: The power of observation and reflexive practice. *Talking Points, 22*(2), 22–28. Reprinted with permission of National Council of Teachers of English (NCTE).

Chapter 7 excerpts from previously published article: Kuby, C.R., 2013. Critical inquiry as relational in early childhood? A teacher's reflection on curriculum, language, and social action. *Voices of Practitioners*. Copyright © 2013 NAEYC. Reprinted with permission.

Chapter 8 excerpts from Pahl, K., & Rowsell, J., 2012. *Literacy and education* (2nd ed.) Thousand Oaks, CA: Sage. Reprinted with permission.

Library of Congress Cataloging-in-Publication Data

Kuby, Candace R.
Critical literacy in the early childhood classroom : unpacking histories, unlearning privilege / Candace R. Kuby, foreword by Vivian M. Vasquez.
    pages cm.—(Language and literacy series)
    Includes bibliographical references and index.
    ISBN 978-0-8077-5469-6 (pbk.)—ISBN 978-0-8077-5470-2 (hardcover)
    1. Language arts (Elementary)—Social aspects. 2. Literacy—Social aspects. 3. Critical pedagogy. I. Title.
    LB1576.K79 2013
    372.6—dc23

                                                                    2013025771

ISBN 978-0-8077-5469-6 (paper)
ISBN 978-0-8077-5470-2 (hardcover)

Printed on acid-free paper
Manufactured in the United States of America

20 19 18 17 16 15 14 13   8 7 6 5 4 3 2 1

To family, friends, and children, who have and continue to inspire and spark moments of consciousness-raising in me.

Contents

Foreword

There is no such thing as a neutral text and there are no such things as neutral teaching practices. Texts and teaching practices are socially constructed and shaped by the theoretical, ideological, cultural, moral, and ethical positions that we embody. Whether we realize it or not, every word that we utter and every action that we take in the classroom involves a choice. Each choice shapes our ways of being and doing in the classroom and the perspectives from which we speak (Vasquez, 2004, 2010). These choices also affect the children we teach, influencing what they can say, what they can do, and ultimately who they can and cannot be. Sometimes these ideological positions are invisible to us; they become normalized ways of being. As such we need to consciously make an effort to continuously reflect on and unpack the positions from which we participate in the world, because these positions help shape what, how, and why we do things in the classroom.

To be literate as a teacher includes engaging in ongoing and sometimes unsettling dialogue with others (Lytle, 2013). This unsettling dialogue can create opportunities for us to consider the positions and perspectives from which we choose to participate in the world. It can help us outgrow our current selves. In this book Candace Kuby places herself in a position of vulnerability in order to make visible her journey of outgrowing her current self. Throughout we witness her attempts at confronting her Whiteness by using an autoethnographic process (Ellis & Bochner, 2006; Spry, 2001). She takes artifacts from her privileged childhood in a White, middle-class family, as well as from her teaching, in creating narrative moments of consciousness from her past. She uses these moments to help de-center her current self, to unpack the choices she has made, and to examine how she may have had her hand in the proverbial cookie jar when it comes to issues of race, class, gender, and social justice. This was hard work, as seen in the challenges and frustrations she describes in the very personal stories she shares.

One such story unfolds while Candace was an elementary school student in Alabama, where she learned about classrooms of African American kindergarten children segregated from the rest of the children in her school. In retrospect she wonders what held her back from problematizing this injustice and asks herself whether her lack of response was rooted in her upbringing. She then wonders how she may have contributed to this inequity by not raising her concern and then considers how these moments from her past influence her teaching today. I see this as both a courageous and confident move: courageous in that it could not have been easy to make public some very personal stories that make her vulnerable, and confident in that she knows what kinds of choices she wants to make to support her students. She's willing to make herself vulnerable while figuring out how to negotiate spaces for exploring important social issues with them. Subsequently, as she attempts to build a critical literacy curriculum drawn from the interests of her students, she wonders, given her past, whether what she identifies as their interests are really her unresolved interests from the past. These moments of uncertainty and critical questioning are evident throughout.

Although there are growing accounts of critical literacy in practice (Comber & Nixon, 2004; Evans, 2004; Vasquez, 2004), I am unaware of anyone who has attempted to create spaces for critical literacy in a setting such as that chosen by Candace. She has created a new space to make visible the importance of critical literacy for all children, including children who are privileged and children who are in alternative school settings, such as the 6-week half-day enrichment program where Candace did her research. While some may see the context as problematic, I choose to see the glass half full. What Candace shows us is that critical literacy is for all children and that critical literacies are ways of being that cut across time and space and move beyond the four walls of the classroom, beyond the "regular" school year. What might you learn about yourself through Candace's journey? How might you use her experience to create spaces for negotiating critical literacies in your setting?

—*Vivian M. Vasquez*

REFERENCES

Comber, B., & Nixon, H. (2004) Children re-read and re-write their local neighborhoods: Critical literacies and identity work. In J. Evans (Ed.), *Literacy moves on* (pp. 115–133). Suffolk, UK: David Fulton Publishers.

Ellis, C., & Bochner, A. (2006). Analyzing analytic autoethnography: An autopsy. *Ethnography, 35*(4), 429–449.

Evans, J. (Ed.). (2004). *Literacy moves on.* Suffolk, UK: David Fulton Publishers.

Lytle, S. (2013). *The critical literacies of teaching.* In C. Kosnik, J. Rowsell, P. Williamson, Simon, R., & Beck, C. (Eds.), *Literacy teacher educators: Preparing teachers for a changing world* (pp. xv–xix). Boston, MA: Sense Publishers.

Spry, T. (2001). Performing autoethnography: An embodied methodological praxis. *Qualitative Inquiry, 7*(6), 706–732.

Vasquez, V. (2004). *Negotiating critical literacy with young children*. New York, NY: Routledge.

Vasquez, V. (2010). *Getting beyond "I like the book": Creating spaces for critical literacy in K–6 settings*. Newark, DE: International Reading Association.

Preface

In the midst of writing this book, two experiences reinforced my beliefs about examining critical moments in our lives that shape how we teach. The first was reading the novel *The Help* by Kathryn Stockett (2009). Set in the 1960s, this novel chronicles the complex relationships of Blacks and Whites living in Mississippi, specifically the quest of a young White woman to interview a range of Black women who serve as "the help" in homes. While Stockett acknowledges that this text is a work of fiction, it is historical fiction, and she explains in an afterword how people such as her family maid Demetrie influenced her life growing up in Mississippi.

Stockett, having moved away from her home in Mississippi, was living in New York City at the time she wrote the novel. As a native of the Deep South, I strongly resonate with Stockett's account of how people respond to her when they ask, "Where are you from?" When she states "Mississippi," she then waits for a response:

> To people who smiled and said, "I've heard it's beautiful down there," I'd say, "My hometown is number three in the nation for gang-related murders." To people who said, "God, you must be glad to be out of that place," I'd bristle and say, "What do you know? It's beautiful down there." (p. 449)

She goes on to explain that once while at a party, a drunk, rich, White man sneered and said, "I am so sorry," when she responded that she was from Mississippi. Stockett writes how she nailed down his foot with her stiletto and proceeded to educate him for 10 minutes on all the famous historical figures that came from Mississippi, such as Oprah Winfrey, William Faulkner, Elvis Presley, and B.B. King, to name a few. Some of her life experiences remind me very much of my own, as I, too, have moved out of the South and typically get reactions of "I'm so sorry," if not verbally, then through the looks on people's faces when I tell them I am from Alabama.

Investing myself emotionally was necessary for the teaching and researching needed to write this book. Exposing my histories and cultures makes me vulnerable to readers and has the potential of hurting those closest to me. I found myself feeling, in Stockett's words, that "Mississippi is like my mother. I am allowed to complain about her all I want, but God help the person who raises an ill word about her around me, unless she is their mother too" (2009, p. 450).

Alabama is home for me. While I am not proud of the issues of race and the struggle for civil rights in my history, I acknowledge that piece of me and work daily to be aware of how my position, privilege, and power reify oppressive structures in society. Much like Stockett's childhood growing up in Mississippi, I, too, witnessed segregation and injustices as a child. This supports my belief that critical conversations are necessary even with our youngest, because they, too, are experiencing and witnessing injustices; giving them permission and a space for dialogue in schools is crucial.

It is important to note that *The Help* was criticized because it is a story about African Americans told through the perspective of a White woman. This relates to my book, as one could perceive it as another text about positioning and power through the lens of a White person. It is. However, while I acknowledge this criticism, it is necessary for people of privilege to examine their position in society. If not, how will things ever change? Writing about Others through the lens of a White woman can both be problematic and provide opportunities at the same time.

A second experience that spoke to me was my visit to an exhibit at the Missouri History Museum and the traveling display "Race: Are We So Different?," created by the American Anthropological Association. The information and images as a whole were amazing and quite humbling to read. However, the one experience that sticks out the most was a 50-minute video, *Race* (American Anthropological Association, 2008), that my husband and I sat down to watch. Standing behind him, I envisioned watching it for a few minutes and then progressing on to the next station. However, I was quickly enthralled, and sat down as a series of Americans shared their stories related to race. The stories ranged from a mixed Black/White couple with a child, to a woman who was adopted at a young age from South Korea, to a White man who grew up in the South with distinctive memories of the oppression African Americans faced. While the narratives were in and of themselves moving, the point that stuck out to me most was that in each story the person shared at least one memory from their childhood that shaped their identity in relation to race. Many of these experiences took place in their early childhood years. As one man said, he knew immediately while witnessing an injustice as a child that something was not right; however, it took him 30 to 40 years to really unpack what happened in that moment. As a child, he suppressed his gut feeling because as a White male he benefited from oppressing another man, a Black man, which seemed normal or expected in his community.

This not only relates to my childhood memories, as shared in the vignettes throughout this book, but it speaks to the need for educators to examine their histories as well as the need for critical conversations with children. We cannot as a society pretend any longer that teaching is neutral. It is not. Teaching decisions are influenced by our histories, experiences, discourses, moments of witnessing, and cultures. We cannot as a society pretend any longer that we need to protect children or that they do not experience and witness injustices. They do. And not only in the South. We must find ways to have critical conversations with children so that over time social action is embodied in them in hopes of a more just world.

My intention is twofold in writing my experiences as shared in this book. Primarily, I hope to urge educators to immerse themselves in *autoethnographic* processes as a way to examine how their ideologies and experiences shape their teaching and researching. Autoethnography is a process of looking inward at the self in order to bring about outward change. Examples of autoethnographic processes are shared throughout the book and in appendices C and D. And second, I hope to urge adults to make room for the voices and experiences of young children, to help them critically read their world. My goal is to provide a glimpse into one way that critical conversations might look with children. As Martin Luther King Jr. wrote in reference to the bus boycott in Alabama: "This movement was not just about desegregating the busses, or even just the mistreatment of our people in Montgomery. This movement was about slaking the centuries-old thirst of a long-suffering people for freedom, dignity, and human rights. It was time to drink at the well" (Carson & Shepard, 2001, p. 5).

It is time for children to drink at the well, too. We must listen to their stories, and our own stories, as a way for us all to learn about our world and move toward a more just society.

Acknowledgments

Writing a book that examines and exposes my position, privilege, and power in society is not easy. As Bolton (2001) writes: "I have come to realize through the process of writing about this incident that reflection is not a *cosy* process of quiet contemplation. It is an active, dynamic, often threatening process, which demands total involvement of self and a commitment to action. In reflective practice there is nowhere to hide" (p. 82, emphasis in original).

Even though there is no place to hide, I found that learning alongside teachers about critical literacy—both preservice and practicing—sparked a flame in me. I found that many educators are open to the ideas of critical literacy even with our youngest learners. However, some are opposed and will not even entertain the notion that children (and people in general) need to dialogue about social issues, much less accept that they might actually be contributing to the oppression of people and ideas. At one time, I was one of these people.

But through years of unpacking my own beliefs, experiences, and memories—many times in community with others—my perspectives changed. As Bolton (2001) posits, "Sharing stories with each other must be one of the best ways of exploring and understanding experience" (p. 10). This book is just that—a way of sharing and exploring my understandings—in hope of sparking the same process in you.

Explorations of the self happened in relation to other people. I acknowledge those who influence who I am as a researcher, writer, teacher, daughter, wife, mother, sister, colleague, friend, and citizen of this world.

During my doctoral program at Indiana University, scholars and mentors of the highest caliber surrounded me. They challenged me to think deeply about my research and teaching as well as how I want to contribute to various communities and participate in social action. Mitzi Lewison, James Damico, Barbara Dennis, Karen Wohlwend, and Gerald Campano taught, inspired, and mentored me, each in unique ways.

I am not sure how I would have made it through this autoethnographic process without the deep friendship and wisdom of Sarah Vander Zanden. She challenged me to clearly articulate my thinking and helped me to craft my writing voice. I am so grateful for her fine-grained reading of my writing. She thoughtfully offered constructive and critical feedback for each chapter.

There are many other educators whom I call friends who have inspired my journey as a teacher researcher. Maryann Manning, Jerry Aldridge, and Lynn Kirkland each played crucial roles in the years of my undergraduate and master's programs at the University of Alabama at Birmingham. They are probably not aware how their lives and interactions have shaped me. Thanks, Lynn, for inviting me back during the summer of 2008 to teach in the enrichment program, as it allowed me to capture and share the stories of the children in this book.

Averee Kirkland Patton, a close friend and colleague, was the ear I went to as a classroom teacher when needing advice. She has a depth of knowledge and understanding about teaching young children. Averee is the voice who grounds me in the real world of teaching when I many times feel detached from it as a university faculty member.

To the faculty at the various elementary schools where I taught and to all the Japanese sensei(s) whom I had the pleasure and honor of learning beside while teaching in Japan, each year of teaching moved me forward in my thinking. Thank you. For those friends who are not educators yet educated me and expanded my beliefs on life and learning, who might find themselves captured in the stories in this book, thank you. Your friendships and wisdom nourish me.

As a child, I never imagined being a writer. Needless to say, I am grateful for the team of editors who positively shaped how this book unfolded. I am indebted to Celia Genishi and Donna Alvermann, peer reviewers' comments, and the virtuosity of Meg Lemke, Emily Spangler, Alison Daltroy, and the production team of Teachers College Press. Each of their insights gave direction to the story I wanted to tell and brought my writing to life.

This book is emotionally rooted in childhood experiences, specifically in relation to my immediate family. I know they will each find themselves in my writing; know that I am continually grateful for my interactions, experiences, and relationships with each of you. It seems trite to try to capture in one or two sentences the gratitude I have for family; however, I will attempt to express my appreciation. Thanks to my mother and father, for loving me unconditionally. Mom, I appreciate the love you give and the bond we share as fellow early childhood educators; the wisdom I gain from your years of experience is invaluable. Dad, although you are a man of few words, I have watched you closely for years and have learned from your actions how to love others and balance life with work and rest. To my sister, your passion for music has encouraged me to welcome the melodies life brings my way and to go after "what nature has intended for me to be." To my brother, your spontaneity with life challenges me to embrace life to the fullest and your humor always brings a smile to my face.

And to Nick, the one who knows and understands me best, you are supportive in ways I could not imagine. Not only am I grateful for the hours you listened to me talk about my teaching/researching, but also for the hours spent editing my writing. Thank you for being more than willing, for offering before I could ask, to clean, cook, wash laundry, and so on more than your fair share in my moments when I felt pressured by deadlines. I know you will find yourself throughout my writing, as our conversations over the years shape who I am in more ways than I can count. Thank you, Nick, for living in the present with me. And to Carlann, my newest joy, I have so much to learn from/with you.

Introduction

The research and writing for this book span a 6-year period from 2008 to 2013. It began with autoethnographic writings and analysis (described in Chapters 1 and 2). As I read books and articles about critical literacy, especially Vivian Vasquez's (2004) book on negotiating inquiries with children, I was struck by the notion of critical literacy as lived. If I was going to live out critical literacy in my teaching as well as life in general, then it made sense that I needed to closely examine myself—my beliefs, assumptions, ideologies, experiences, and memories. When the opportunity to go back into the classroom during the summer of 2008 to teach young children presented itself, I knew I wanted to be intentional, to listen closely to students' actions and conversations for possible critical literacy inquiries for us to explore.

While teaching, I collected a variety of data (e.g., audio and video recordings of whole-class, small-group, and one-on-one interactions; student-made artwork and writings; class-made books; parental questionnaires; my daily audio reflection journal; teaching notes and plans; and photographs). The students represented a diverse range of races and ethnicities, but for the most part the children came from relatively affluent homes. During the summer, I listened to video and audio recordings of classroom interactions to plan for the next learning engagements with children.

After the summer program concluded, I spent 2 years as a graduate student analyzing data closely for aspects of emotion in critical literacy (Kuby, 2010, 2013c), with crystallization as an overarching methodology (Ellingson, 2009; Kuby, in press). Specifically, I studied how emotions are performed in critical literacy conversations and actions, drawing on narrative (Riessman, 2008), critical sociocultural (Lewis, Enciso, & Moje, 2007), and rhizomatic theories (Deleuze & Guattari, 1987). While narrative and sociocultural theories are more prominent in educational research, rhizomatic theory is less common. Rhizomatic theory draws on the scholarship of French philosophers Deleuze and Guattari (1987). A rhizome is a root structure that instead of growing linearly breaks off in shoots and grows in new, unexpected directions. Examples of rhizomes include bulbs and tubers such as Bermuda grass, ginger, irises, ferns, and asparagus. Rhizomatic theory allowed me to analyze the nonlinearity of emotions and departures

1

(or unexpected directions) from traditional interactions in an early childhood classroom. In the process of analysis, I juxtaposed autoethnographic writings with data from classroom interactions.

Several additional years revisiting the data led to the draft of this book. During these years I read numerous publications on Whiteness theory,[1] which sparked me to analyze my life experiences and teaching decisions again. This additional time to think about teaching interactions resulted in the broad insight categories that I titled "moments of consciousness-raising," as captured in Chapters 4 to 8.

During these years I also taught literacy methods courses for preservice early childhood and elementary majors. I struggled (and still do) with how to teach them about critical literacy without making critical literacy seem like a checklist of questions to ask after read-alouds. How do you make critical literacy something students live, as Vasquez (2004) writes? From this struggle, I began to incorporate autoethnographic processes (as described in the appendixes) with readings and learning engagements on the pedagogy of critical literacy. This is still a practice I reflect on and refine each semester.

Even though the writing for this book is finished, the reflection and revisiting of data continue. I intentionally weave questions through the book not only to ask the reader to think with me, but also to demonstrate the evolving stories and identities we have. Many of the questions included are still unanswered. As McIntyre (1997) states, she never discovered "right answers" to the questions that surfaced as she made her Whiteness public: "I believe that the most important questions are those that resist a simple, factual, individual answer. There are/were no simple answers to racism, neither are/were there simple strategies for being a white participant-researcher investigating the meaning of whiteness with a group of white student teachers" (p. 29).

The tensions of unanswered questions are productive.

OVERVIEW OF THIS BOOK

The book is divided into two parts. Part I, consisting of Chapters 1 through 3, unpacks my histories and journey as a teacher/researcher. In this section, I also contextualize my history, the theoretical perspectives informing teaching and research, the summer program, the children, and the critical literacy inquiry (all names of students and teachers are pseudonyms).

Part II, consisting of Chapters 4 through 9, examines pivotal moments of consciousness-raising in relation to teaching. I juxtapose conversations from teaching with vignettes from my childhood, casting a critical perspective on the interactions. Through autoethnographic writing I wrestle with global discourses and issues of power and agency that shaped my upbringing and teaching decisions.

In Part II I also discuss insights I gained as a teacher researcher. I share the reflexive, and many times difficult, journey of a critical educator. Even though moments of consciousness-raising can be trying, I encourage educators to view these tensions as productive.

Part I: Histories, Contexts, Ideologies, and Pedagogical Beliefs

Chapter 1 discusses theoretical perspectives and methodologies that shape my teaching/researching. Specifically, I explore autoethnography, critical literacy, critical sociocultural theory, and Whiteness theory.

In Chapter 2, I share several photographs and critical narrative events from my upbringing to demonstrate how these histories influenced my beliefs and teaching. This chapter contextualizes my history growing up in the southern United States and my experiences related to race, class, religion, and other social issues. I discuss my social construction of privilege as a child, which the rest of the book builds on.

I frame my own process of consciousness-raising with literature on autoethnography. Autoethnographies come from a process of looking closely at personal narratives and experiences that bring light to a teacher's lived, historical experiences (Ellis & Bochner, 2006; Jones, 2005, 2007; Spry, 2001), in this case related to social injustices. Drawing on Whiteness (Giroux, 1997; McIntyre, 1997; McLaren & Muñoz, 2000; Tatum, 1999) and critical theories (Freire, 1970/2005; Kincheloe & McLaren, 2005), I take a critical perspective on several memories from my childhood.

Framed as teacher research (Cochran-Smith & Lytle, 1993, 2009) using ethnographic methods, in Chapter 3 I contextualize the summer program, describing the city, school district, and students, and give an overview of the critical literacy curriculum. I share my history within this community and intentions going into teaching. I introduce the incident at the heart of our critical literacy inquiry, when students were told that playground benches were for adults only.

Part II: Moments of Consciousness-Raising

In Part II, I discuss examples from my childhood and teaching that demonstrate moments of consciousness-raising. Questions that guided the inquiry process and writing are:

1. What are my moments of consciousness-raising?
2. How do these moments connect to my histories, ideologies, and beliefs about teaching?
3. What was I reinforcing or reifying (stereotypes, positions in society, beliefs, etc.) in the moments of teaching?

4. What was I doing intentionally as a teacher and what was I not
    aware of?

Moments of consciousness-raising were not always apparent in the act
of teaching; instead, many surfaced later, when I had time to closely examine the interactions and my decisions. The chapters in Part II contain
descriptions from teaching interactions, excerpts from my teaching journal,
student art, and transcripts[2] of conversations. I pair these with flashbacks
and images from my childhood and attempt to unpack these experiences using Whiteness and critical theories. I discuss five areas: witnessing (Chapter
4), Whiteness (Chapter 5), negotiated critical literacy curriculum (Chapter
6), language (Chapter 7), and social action (Chapter 8). In the final chapter,
I reflect on tensions I experienced and posit that consciousness-raising is an
ongoing process.

In Chapter 4, I explore the tensions of witnessing inequities through
the lens of what happened when teachers[3] told my students to get off the
playground bench, coupled with experiences I witnessed related to social
injustices as a child. What does someone do with what they see, experience,
and know? At times, I felt it was almost better to not know. But once you
do know, you have to do something with it. How do we talk with children
about inequities they have witnessed?

In Chapter 5, I draw on Whiteness and critical theories to explore how
my histories and ideologies shaped curricular decisions in the critical literacy
inquiry. I draw on conversation around read-alouds about Rosa Parks coupled with experiences from my elementary school years, discovering classes
of African American kindergarten students in the basement of my citywide
magnet school. I ponder questions such as: Did the critical topics I chose to
bring back to the class for discussion reinforce privileges and assumptions of
Whiteness? What did it mean for me to connect the playground experience
with Parks's bus arrest?

In Chapter 6, I explore the idea of a negotiated critical literacy curriculum. While it is my belief that curriculum should be co-created with
children, it is worthwhile to closely examine what that looks like in practice,
tangled in a web of power relationships and ideologies. While teaching I
grappled with how much to say about my own beliefs in relation to segregation and the playground bench incident. I wondered if I was being dogmatic
or trying to force the children to see multiple viewpoints. I share excerpts
from my teaching journal to demonstrate the constant struggle in negotiating a critical literacy curriculum with students and how the decisions are
connected to a teacher's ideologies.

In Chapter 7, I explore the language I used with young children around
issues of segregation, racism, and power between teacher and students. The
language I chose to use connected to the labels I heard as a child growing up

in the South. Terms such as White, Black, and Brown were used to describe groups of people. Did this reinforce the misunderstanding of race equaling a skin color, rather than as something socially constructed? While teaching, I struggled with words such as "we" and "they" in reference to events we discussed about segregation. Language is not neutral (Street, 1984), and as educators it is crucial to become aware of how language positions and has the potential to hurt people.

In Chapter 8, I explore what social action is in a critical literacy curriculum, especially with young children. Most scholarship focuses on the larger social action projects such as creating petitions or surveys, acting out a drama to share various viewpoints on an issue, or planning an event in a community with various people who hold positions of power—all worthy endeavors. I questioned if social action could occur in subtler, embodied ways over time and spaces. I noticed that social action related to events in my childhood, such as how my discovery of racially segregated kindergarten classes in my elementary school did not become social action until years later as an adult, when I contemplated these experiences and allowed them to change how I thought and interacted with people of different races. Were there embodied moments of social action in the critical literacy inquiry, such as in paintings or spontaneous role-play?

Chapter 9 aims to discuss how the tensions of teaching from a critical literacy stance, shared in Chapters 4 through 8, coupled with autoethnographic processes, is difficult yet productive. I encourage educators to take the time and emotional energy needed to embark on autoethnographic journeys to better understand their own ideologies and how they shape teaching and/or researching.

Teaching (and researching) from a critical stance is not always easy. In this final chapter, I share examples, specifically from my teaching journal, that support the tensions and uncertainty that come from listening to children and attempting to foster spaces for critical literacy.

Finally, in the appendixes, I share resources that educators can use to encourage preservice teachers, inservice teachers, graduate students, and themselves to embark on autoethnographic journeys. As I teach literacy methods courses for preservice teachers and graduate seminars for doctoral students on research, I make an effort to weave autoethnographic discussions and experiences throughout the courses. I am still in process of discovering ways to engage my students, many of whom are Caucasian, middle-class females, in productive ways to experience moments of consciousness-raising and consider how their identities and ideologies shape teaching and/or researching decisions. Identifying moments of consciousness-raising is necessary work for educators. I invite readers to reflect on their own moments of consciousness-raising.

NOTES

1. Throughout the book I capitalize White and Black, as Whiteness scholar Tatum (1999) does. I do this to indicate a race of people tied to multiple identities, not simply a description of skin tone or color. By doing this, I acknowledge that race is socially constructed, not biological. I also kept the language of White and Black in audio reflection journal entries, vignettes from childhood, and classroom conversations to reflect what was said in the moment. Throughout analysis, I use the terms *African American* and *Caucasian*.

2. Most transcriptions from classroom conversations and audio reflection journal entries are typed word for word. However, sometimes my language in reflective journals was not succinct and for the purpose of this book, I chose to clean up the transcription for easier readability. In some cases, I intentionally left the transcript as is to demonstrate a point (e.g., use of modal words, long pauses for hesitancy, etc.). In the transcripts, I use parenthesis enclosed with numbers to represent the number of seconds a pause lasted (e.g., (4) means a 4-second pause). I use an ellipses (e.g., . . .) to indicate when I omitted sections of the conversations.

3. As indicated in reflective journal entries, the incident on the playground involved more than one teacher. However, the one teacher who vocalized that the bench was for adults only was Mrs. Adams. Other teachers were with her on the bench but did not vocalize their opinion on the matter. Thus, in classroom conversations, we discussed the inequity in relation to Mrs. Adams. As teachers had the choice of the number of weeks to teach in the summer program, many were not there all 6 weeks. The first incident with the teachers regarding the bench happened in the first 2 weeks of the program. Another incident solely with Mrs. Adams happened during the last week of the program.

Part I

HISTORIES, CONTEXTS, IDEOLOGIES, AND PEDAGOGICAL BELIEFS

CHAPTER 1

Theories and Methodologies of Consciousness-Raising

> We write before knowing what to say and how to say it, and in order to
> find out, if possible. (Lyotard, 1992, p. 103)

Growing up as a White, middle-class female in the southern United States in the 1980s and 1990s, with its strong history of segregation, poverty, and the struggle for civil rights, as well as in a heavily conservative, religious environment, left me with a lot of processing to do as I have grown older. While I deeply love and value the people from my childhood, whether within my family or in relationships at school, church, or extracurricular activities, my now-expanded view of the world has left me with questions. Why were some children in my elementary school segregated to the basement? Why did my church feel the need to go on trips to "save the souls" of primarily marginalized and oppressed groups of people? Why did religion and the rationalizing of injustices so often overlap? Why can I not remember ever having a "person of color" in my home as a child? What led to my fear of other races and my discomfort regarding cultural activities and discourses that were different from mine? Why did people, when describing a situation with an African American person, preface the narrative with "the Black" but never saw the need to preface other stories with "the White"? These questions and experiences, and the memories associated with them, affect my life and shape the educator I am.

The purpose of this book is to share my journey as a teacher researcher (Cochran-Smith & Lytle, 1993, 2009) unpacking my beliefs, ideologies, and histories. Unpacking is a process of closely examining and exploring what makes up a person's worldview, the experiences, conversations, memories, and traditions that create a person's paradigm. Using the plurals of *ideology, belief,* and *history,* connotes the complex, fluid, and multiple aspects of a person. As Freire (1970/2005) writes, moments of critical consciousness-raising help us focus on understanding the world and the word for social and political contradictions. Freire describes the dialogical relationship between the world and words—knowledge about texts is also knowledge about the world. Texts defined broadly include books (or other written materials) but also pop culture, media, songs, art, and gestures. It is through consciousness-raising that action can happen to change power dynamics in relationships.

I intentionally juxtapose experiences teaching, primarily during a summer enrichment program with 5- and 6-year-olds, with my life histories. It is not possible, or even desirable, for educators to attempt to keep the personal out of teaching and/or researching. Therefore, we need to critically unpack pivotal moments in our lives. Let us be mindful in illuminating, confronting, and unpacking our ideologies and experiences. While the process of examining our histories might be painful or uncomfortable, it is necessary (Jacobson, 2003).

In this chapter I discuss theoretical perspectives that guide my thinking and writing: critical literacy, critical sociocultural theory, and Whiteness theory. I begin with a discussion on autoethnography and writing as a method of inquiry—both as theoretical perspectives and as methodologies for unpacking ideologies and experiences.

AUTOETHNOGRAPHY

The personal narratives throughout the book come from several years of intentionally writing as a form of inquiry (Richardson & St. Pierre, 2005). Using an autoethnographic process, I wrote personal narratives in response to questions prompting me to unpack conversations and memories from my childhood and young adult years. Autoethnography is a process of composing self-narratives that critique the situatedness of self with others in social contexts (Spry, 2001). Two overarching points from various autoethnography scholars are that (1) context is crucial, because narratives are embedded in interactions, and (2) autoethnography is not self-serving but has a goal of social action (Atkinson & Delamont, 2006; Cole & Knowles, 2001; Jones, 2007; Muncey, 2005). I encourage educators to envision ways of using autoethnographic processes in courses with preservice teachers and graduate students and in their own lives to create social change. In the appendixes, I share examples of self-interview questions and ways of using writing, art, conversation, and media to facilitate autoethnographic processes.

Autoethnography as a Process of Consciousness-Raising

Within teaching, specifically from a critical literacy perspective, there is a need for teachers to intentionally examine who they are and how their beliefs shape teaching decisions. A methodology of autoethnography is one way to examine personal narratives from a critical stance with the goal of bringing to consciousness belief systems that shape our practice and changing the way we teach for more just relationships. Autoethnographies (Ellis & Bochner, 2006; Jones, 2005, 2007; Spry, 2001) come from a process of looking closely at personal narratives that can bring to light a teacher's lived, historical experiences, in this case related to social injustices. Drawing on Whiteness theory (Giroux, 1997; McIntyre, 1997; McLaren & Muñoz, 2000; Tatum, 1999) and other critical scholars (Freire, 1970/2005; Kincheloe & McLaren, 2005), I take a critical perspective on memories from my childhood. Autoethnography is a process that supports the living out of critical literacy.

The purpose of autoethnography is to achieve critical agency in attempting to know oneself through critiquing and sharing one's own experience (Duncan, 2004; Spry, 2001). Critical agency is when action, consciousness-raising, and change come from the autoethnographic experience. Jones (2003) states:

> Autoethnographies also move from the inside of the author to outward expression while working to take readers inside themselves and ultimately out again. Readers and audiences are invited to share in the emotional experience of an author . . . In telling their stories, autoethnographers ask readers to embark on a collaborative journey that tacks between individual experience and social roles, relationships, and structures. (p. 115)

Autoethnographies are not self-serving but have the goal of changing the world (Ellis & Bochner, 2006; Jones, 2005). Autoethnographies embrace the life of a researcher (and teacher) as multilayered and worthy of expression (Duncan, 2004).

Stories as a Way of Understanding and Constructing Our World

Drawing on the scholarship of Richardson and St. Pierre (2005), writing is viewed as a method of inquiry. In this stance, "writing is validated as a method of knowing" (p. 962). The work of Bolton (2001) in the book *Reflective Practice: Writing and Professional Development* advocates much like the scholarship of Richardson and St. Pierre (2005), for instructors of nurses, educators, doctors, and lawyers to habitually engage in the act of writing as a way to critically unpack their stories. Bolton (2010) writes, "Stories are the mode we use to make sense of our world and ourselves" (p. 7). Bolton argues that reflective practice through writing is not only an individual experience but should be shared with others. Bolton (2010) states:

A story is an attempt to create order and security out of a chaotic world. . . .
But for our experiences to develop us—socially, psychologically, spiritually—
our world must be made to appear strange. We, and our students, must be
encouraged to examine our story-making processes critically: to create and rec-
reate fresh accounts of our lives from different perspectives, different points of
view . . . and we must elicit and listen to the responses of peers. . . . Effective reflective practice meets the paradoxical need both to tell and retell our stories in
order for us to feel secure enough, and yet critically examine our actions, and
those of others, in order dynamically to increase our understanding of ourselves
and our practice, and *develop dynamically.* (pp. 9–10, emphasis in original)

Autoethnography and Bolton's (2001, 2010) scholarship are closely
related because autoethnography is a retrospective account involving reflexivity and voice of the writer (Duncan, 2004; Wall, 2006). The author
looks inward and creates a reflective dialogue with readers stemming from
their lived experiences in order to share with others and engage in social
change (Humphreys, 2005). Writing is a way to unpack stories across time
and spaces and intentionally try to understand ideologies, experiences, and
memories that influence teaching, learning, and researching.

However, narratives are not merely reflections of what someone does in
the world or past experiences; instead, narratives describe what the world
does to a person and create experiences for their audiences. Within schools,
interactions can be read as narratives. For example, children playing together, a dialogue between a teacher and student, and a conversation after a book
is read aloud can all be read as a narrative event. Educators can explore children's talk, art, writing, performance, and interactions as narratives.

Drawing on narrative scholarship (Alvermann, 2000; Riessman, 2008),
I use the notion of critical narrative events. Webster and Mertova (2007)
state that an event "becomes critical when it has the 'right mix of ingredi-
ents at the right time and in the right context'" (p. 73). They go on to write:
"[W]hat makes a critical event 'critical' is the impact it has on the storyteller.
It is almost always a change experience, and it can only ever be identified
afterwards . . . critical events are 'critical' because of their impact and profound effect on whoever experiences such an event. They often bring about
radical change in the person. These events are unplanned, unanticipated and
uncontrolled" (pp. 74, 77).

The stories I selected to write about have had a profound impact on
me. As I revisited data from teaching and the written narratives from my
childhood, stories continued to surface as pivotal moments of interactions. I
chose pivotal events not only because they seemed to shape the interactions
I had with students and our curriculum, but also because they stuck with
me. I acknowledge that the classroom conversations captured on audio and
video files as well as photographs of student-made artifacts only partially

give voice to students' stories (and those of other teachers). I am selecting and crafting the narratives; I see myself as the storyteller.

Most of the classroom examples discussed in this book come from a summer of teaching 5- and 6-year-old children in an enrichment program in the South. I am a White female who was raised in an middle-class family. Like my students, I also grew up in the Deep South. Based on the parental questionnaires, many of the students seemed to be raised with conservative religious beliefs, as I was. Since I left my childhood home, my viewpoints on issues related to politics, religion, racism, and other social issues have evolved. My prior experiences and interactions shaped the decisions I made as a teacher, which is more fully discussed in the remaining chapters.

As a practitioner researcher, I felt it was important to closely reflect on my life experiences (Campano, 2007; Glesne, 2005), which influence my thinking on social issues and could shape curricular activities and discussions with children. It is important as a person of relative privilege to try to understand my relation to people who are systematically marginalized in my community and the world. It was my hope that through the process of autoethnography, I would have an awareness and understanding that would influence *how* and *what* I did with young children while teaching. Consciousness-raising in and of itself is not enough; taking action is important. As a teacher I knew my actions related to curriculum decisions and conversations with children would need to change after an autoethnographic process. Through reflections and analysis of classroom interactions, I attempted to understand, as much as I could, how my position and values as a White, middle-class woman affected curriculum decisions.

I resonate with Smith (2005), who wonders how she can best gain knowledge about herself and how her experience affects what she observes and researches. I strive to deconstruct borders of my identity as a teacher, researcher, author, doctoral student, wife, daughter, sister, mother, and so on (Humphreys, 2005). The autoethnographic process gave me a chance to understand how my positions reproduce dominant ideologies in society, and also to challenge multiple, simultaneous positions (e.g., race, gender, education, age, class, religion, etc.) and begin a process of consciousness-raising. My hope is that through sharing this journey with others they, too, will reflect on their life experiences in relation to their practice.

CRITICAL SOCIOCULTURAL THEORY AND CRITICAL LITERACY

Broadly speaking, I view literacy as social acts (C. Lewis, 2001). Literacy is not neutral, but is complex, fluid, and always takes place in relationship with others, which means that power is inextricably tied to literacy

(Lewis et al., 2007; Street, 1984). As teachers and/or researchers, we can learn from literacy events and practices (Barton & Hamilton, 2000; Bloome, Carter, Christian, Otto, & Shuart-Faris, 2005; Street, 2000) in our lives and classrooms. By focusing on observable events, we can better understand the not-so-obvious literacy practices that involve feelings, values, power, and cultural ways of using literacy.

Lewis et al., (2007) argue:

> [T]he theoretical frameworks currently informing sociocultural research in literacy do not overtly address important issues of identity, agency, and power in the production of knowledge that are central to understanding literacy as a social and cultural practice. . . . Our aim is to generate a sociocultural theory that accounts for these larger systems of power as they shape and are shaped by individuals in particular cultural contexts . . . the field needs what we refer to as "critical sociocultural theory." (p. xi)

In their own scholarship, they have turned to poststructural, cultural, feminist, critical race, and discourse theories to inform their understanding of the social, cultural, mental, physical, and political. Referring to the work of Gutiérrez and Larson (1994), they point out that "sociocultural theory is very useful for understanding the relationship between culture and learning but that the additional framework of critical pedagogy [is] needed to fully understand the relationship between power, ideology, and schooling" (Lewis et al., 2007, p. 3). Critical sociocultural theory questions the dialogic and power-laden aspects of interactions and literacy within local and global D/discourses (Gee, 2005).

A critical sociocultural theory complements a critical literacy approach because this theoretical stance encourages readers to examine interactions, texts, and language in cultural contexts. Critical literacy focuses on people reading their world and the words of texts for issues of power, position, and privilege (Freire 1970/2005). I understand critical literacy as an inquiry process of deconstructing and reconstructing texts (written, spoken, artistic, performed, etc.) for aspects of power, position, and privilege. Therefore, critical literacy is not only for deconstructing but also for envisioning new ways of being and reconstructing the world (McLaren & Muñoz, 2000). Critical literacy is a living, inquiry process, where people ask questions about life, texts, language, and interactions with others and act on new, just ways of being together. Critical literacy is lived (Vasquez, 2004): it is not an add-on to curriculum, but something we actively do, live, and breathe. Critical literacy thus calls for educators to examine their own lives and ideologies.

MOMENTS OF CONSCIOUSNESS-RAISING: UNPACKING HISTORIES
AND IDEOLOGIES WITH WHITENESS THEORY

This book focuses on the intersections of a teacher's ideologies that influenced critical literacy teaching, looking at the process and struggle in becoming a critical literacy teacher and the decisions made while teaching. I look not so much at the critical literacy pedagogy but rather at the complexity of teaching as it tangles with a person's ideologies and histories. In my case, I wrestled with moments in my childhood and young adult years that influenced how I responded to children's questions about racism and other injustices. For example, why was I so disturbed by other teachers' demands that my students not sit on a playground bench? Why did I make a connection to Rosa Parks? How did my own Whiteness shape decisions I made with the curriculum, which students' questions I took up, and which ones I did not make curricular space for over the summer?

Various scholars write about Whiteness and its impact on education (Fine, Weis, Powell, & Wong, 1997; Giroux, 1997; hooks, 1992; Kincheloe, Steinberg, Rodriguez, & Chennault, 1998; A.E. Lewis, 2004; McIntyre, 1997; Tatum, 1999). Whiteness theory scholars articulate the points listed below. These tenets of Whiteness theory guided the analysis of my actions, experiences, and ideologies. These are generalized statements, based on a body of research, not proclamations that all White people believe or enact these ideas. As Tatum (1999) points out (see final bullet point), there is a process in developing a healthy White identity, to which I aspire.

1. Whiteness is seen as an unexamined norm in society. Whites represent the societal norm, and therefore Whites can reach adulthood without thinking much about their racial identity (hooks, 1992; Tatum, 1999).
2. Whites tend to believe that racial identity is something that other people have, not something that is salient for them (Tatum, 1999).
3. Whites tend to think of themselves as individuals and sometimes show frustration at being seen as a group member. This mentality could stem from the dominant ideology of rugged individualism and the American myth of meritocracy. Thinking of one only as an individual, instead of part of multiple identity groups, is the "legacy of White privilege" (Tatum, 1999, p. 102).
4. Whites sometimes recognize their race's power but fail to see its impact on the lives of marginalized groups of people. Whites sometimes fail to understand the experience of surveillance that African Americans (and perhaps other racial groups) have undergone in the United States (McIntyre, 1997).

4. Whiteness in the United States can be understood largely through the social consequences it provides for those who are considered to be nonwhite (McLaren & Muñoz, 2000).

5. There are two major tasks in the process of developing a healthy sense of White identity: (1) abandonment of individual racism and (2) recognition of and opposition to institutional and cultural racism. This happens over six phases: contact, disintegration, reintegration, pseudo-independence, immersion/emersion, and autonomy (Tatum, 1999).

As McLaren and Muñoz (2000) write, "One is not born white but becomes white by virtue of the social context in which one finds oneself, to be sure, but also by virtue of the choices one makes" (p. 41). Therefore, if as educators our goal is not simply tolerance but acceptance of diversity, in this case in regard to race and ethnicity, it is imperative that we begin with an examination, however difficult, of our own lives—looking at aspects of both choice and inheritance. Henry Giroux (1997) eloquently captures the difficultly of this task:

> In order for teachers, students, and others to come to terms with whiteness existentially and intellectually, they need to take up the challenge in our classrooms and across a wide variety of public sites of confronting racism in all its complexity and ideological and material formations. But most important, whiteness must provide a diverse but critical space from which to wage a wider struggle against the many forces that undermine what it means to live in a society founded on the principles of freedom, racial justice, and economic equality. Rewriting whiteness in a discourse of resistance and possibility represents more than a challenge to dominant and progressive notions of racial politics; it offers an import pedagogical challenge for educating cultural workers, teachers, and students to live with and through difference as a defining principle of radical democracy. (p. 313)

Educators play a key role in children's identity formation. However difficult the task, we must examine not only how our race shapes our identities but also how gender, religious experiences, socioeconomic status, family, friends, schooling, and discourses we have heard related to social and political issues such as gender, sexual orientation, war, violence, and people with disabilities affect us. This process of examination is vital to equality, equity, and justice in our society.

As Christine Sleeter (1993) points out, there is a need to make multicultural and critical pedagogy a part of teacher education courses. However, in multicultural and critical literacy pedagogies there is little discussion of

Whiteness (McLaren & Muñoz, 2000; Sleeter, 1993). Some educators have begun the conversation by writing about their own histories in relation to teaching (Ballenger, 1999; Hankins, 2003; Jacobson, 2003). There is a need to explicitly bring Whiteness, and other aspects of identity formation, into the critical literacy discussion. As McLaren and Muñoz (2000) state:

> Even among critical educators, little attention is given to the formation of whiteness. Whiteness is universalized as an identity that both supersedes and transcends ethnicity. . . . We need to recognize that most attempts at practicing a form of multiculturalism actually reconfirm relations of power and privilege. This is because social practices of whiteness are rarely, if ever, named, let alone interrogated in the clarion call for increasing cultural diversity. (p. 35)

This book is an attempt to interweave a critical perspective on Whiteness (and other aspects of identity) directly with critical literacy teaching. While I use Whiteness and critical perspectives to unpack my histories and unlearn my privilege, you are invited to draw on perspectives that best relate to your identities, which could include: critical race theory, ingenious scholarship, feminist perspectives, queer theory, and so forth. My hope is the book demonstrates one way of unpacking identities and unlearning ideologies but realize each of our autoethnographic journeys will look different.

Writing such a book is not easy; going public with the rawness exposed in this text is risky. I resonate with McIntyre's (1997) tensions of making Whiteness public as a teacher researcher: "I also found myself struggling with what I refer to as the politics of engagement and the politics of critique—a complicated and contentious experience that exemplifies what it was like to be a white participant-researcher invoking Freirean principles of consciousness-raising and self-reflection with a group of white participants" (p. 30).

Even though McIntyre was referring to work with preservice teachers, I found similarities in my work with 5- and 6-year-olds who were primarily White. In this book I attempt to make the tensions and unlearning I went through as a teacher researcher transparent in hopes of helping educators and/or researchers, even preservice teachers, begin an autoethnographic process, looking closely at the personal narratives that shape them as people and educators.

I want to be clear that this type of writing is difficult and makes one vulnerable. It is difficult work to write as a White, privileged woman, knowing that others who experience marginalization(s) will critique it. I have heard people say that you cannot understand the life of an African American unless you identify as one. I understand this line of thinking. But this type of thinking can also be problematized on various levels; for example, not all African Americans have the same experiences. Taking an exclusionary stance could perpetuate silence and reinscribe dominant, oppressive beliefs and actions. This is a challenge of writing this book. I not only attempt to unpack my own histories and ideologies but also try to understand how my position has oppressed others, which is neither easy nor comfortable. As McIntyre (1997) writes, "Volunteering to make our whiteness public suggests a willingness on the part of white people to expose our whiteness to critique. . . . Thus, I feel it is necessary that I not only listen to the contributions that people of color can make to my understanding of racism and my positionality within that system, but also join them in cocreating opportunities for critical reflection and dialogue" (p. 42).

I acknowledge up front that words such as "White" and "Black" reinforce the idea that race is biological and perhaps synonymous with skin color. However, I have chosen to keep the language as close to the original from transcripts of conversations with children. I also use these terms in memoir-writing because they are true to the language I heard and used growing up. I now understand race to be a social construction tied to oppression, power, position, and privileges in a culture. The process of teaching, researching, and writing has taught me that I am never finished unpacking histories and ideologies. Each time I listen to recorded conversations from teaching or revisit a memory from my childhood, I learn something new.

CRITICAL LITERACY WITH RELATIVELY AFFLUENT YOUNG CHILDREN?

While there are texts on critical literacy with upper elementary and secondary students (Campano, 2007; Christensen, 1999; Clarke, 2005; Edelsky, 1999; Heffernan & Lewison, 2000, 2003, 2005; Morrell, 2004; Sweeney, 1999), in comparison little is written about critical literacy in the early childhood years. The scholarship of Vivian Vasquez (2001, 2004, 2005), Barbara Comber and colleagues (2001, 2006, 2008), Mary Cowhey (2006), and Mariana Souto-Manning (2009) serves as exemplars that are useful in envisioning what critical literacy might look like in early childhood classrooms. While these are pivotal texts that shape my thinking, I know that adopting a perspective of critical literacy as early childhood curriculum is still uncommon. It took me years of unpacking and examining my own beliefs before I wholeheartedly embraced this type of inquiry with young children. This was not because young children cannot "do" critical literacy, but because I had to work through long-embedded developmental beliefs about early childhood teaching as well as my own ideologies about injustices. As Gerald Campano (2007) writes, "One of our first challenges as teacher researchers is to inquire into and often call into question our own taken-for-granted assumptions about teaching and learning" (p. 12). I had to first ask myself what assumptions I had about teaching and learning in early childhood before becoming (and continuing to be) a critical literacy educator.

After listening to stories of people who experienced oppression, such as those at the museum referenced in the Preface, I typically find a pattern. Most share vivid memories from events in their early childhood years. This helps confirm my belief that critical literacy teaching needs to begin with our youngest learners. They live and experience a world full of injustices; they come to us with a discourse of fairness. There is a need to work with children, especially of privilege, at young ages. If we wait until children become adults, as with many preservice education students when they face critical inquiry for the first time, it becomes more difficult for them to reflect critically on their lives. The system seems to work for them: therefore it is harder for them to understand or see systematic and socially constructed reasons for poverty, racism, homophobia, and the other ways people are not treated as fully human.

Most critical literacy scholarship is focused on children who are considered marginalized for various reasons (i.e., race, class, language, gender, sexual orientation, etc.) and is about empowering marginalized groups to find their voices and places in a society based on the ideologies of dominant groups (Blackburn & Clark, 2007; Campano, 2007; Comber & Simpson, 2001; Edelsky, 1999; Fine, 1997). It is important for marginalized groups to become empowered and stand up to hegemonic practices, and I value and embrace the research done with children of marginalized groups; this is noble and necessary work of helping people to deconstruct their worlds and find ways to speak up. But as an early childhood educator who taught primarily in school districts serving privileged populations, I also see a need for providing affluent young children the spaces to dialogue about injustices in their communities and hopefully, through these conversations, initiate and engage in social change. While this might sound simplistic, hearing the voices of those oppressed is only one piece of social justice work. Those in positions of power and privilege need to understand how their lives and actions, even if unconsciously, oppress others. If this does not happen, oppression will remain and the voices of the marginalized will continue to be met with opposition because those with privilege do not typically want to relinquish power. Members of the group(s) with oppressive and/or domineering power should also have spaces to dialogue about how their power positions affect other people.

Although theoretically I believe that critical literacy teaching is important, I found tensions and questions as I taught. How do we create curricular spaces for children, primarily White but also children of various races who have high economic status, to discuss their positions and privileges in society? So often people with power, position, and privilege in society do not see (or choose not to see) how their lives negatively affect others (Delpit, 1995, 2002; Derman-Sparks & Ramsey, 2011). How do we help students (both early childhood students and preservice teachers) of privilege understand systematic oppression? How do we help students respond to or possibly overcome entitlement thinking? How do we help students not feel guilty, but use their new understandings about oppression to fuel activism and justice for others? How do we help students find ways to reconstruct or dismantle injustices, not participate in them? This type of teaching is not an easy task, but one that is necessary if justice and equity for all is the goal.

Even after reading numerous texts on critical literacy and using it as a pedagogical stance as I teach, I still question what critical literacy is.

1. What does "critical" mean? Does "critical" mean "to agree with me [the teacher]"?
2. What does critical literacy really look like? Do we want students to agree with what we think is critical?
3. Who are the students trying to please with criticality? Is it just about teacher-pleasing, telling me what I want to hear?
4. Are we imposing our power as teachers on students? Am I, as the teacher, *really* critical?

These questions in many ways were catalysts for the close examination of my beliefs and teaching practices, yet even after years of pondering, these questions remain unanswered. As educators we need to be conscious of how the embodiment of our beliefs materializes in teaching interactions and decisions. Whose critical literacy is it anyway?

A NOTE ON CRITICALNESS AND POWER

I want to be clear up front about the term "critical." This book engages multiple kinds of criticalness. One layer is the case study of the critical literacy inquiry that took place during the summer program. In that sense, I refer to inequitable social issues, such as those that prompted the Montgomery bus boycott and the civil rights movement more generally, and the inequity of power that happened on our playground. I used various texts and literacy practices with my students to deconstruct and reconstruct social issues.

Another layer of criticalness relates to the power dynamic between my students and me, among students, and in relation to our conversations about other authority figures (i.e., other teachers). Therefore, many times not only was the content of our dialogues critical but also the very act of conversing as teacher/student about inequities (especially in reference to relationships at school, such as with the teachers on the playground) can be viewed as critical, disrupting traditional power structures in schools. A third layer of criticalness is my use of perspectives such as Whiteness and critical theories (Giroux, 1997; McIntyre, 1997; McLaren & Muñoz, 2000; Tatum, 1999) to unpack my position and privilege in society.

Therefore, I want to preface the book with a brief discussion on power and argue that the insights I gained are helping me to reconceptualize power. As educators, we need to interrogate and nuance power to better understand critical literacy. In the field of critical theory that critical literacy draws on, some see power as binary—composed of the oppressor and the oppressed. In critical theory "Other" denotes a person or group of people viewed as different from those traditionally with power (Hawkesworth, 2007; Said, 1978). Kincheloe and McLaren (2005), conceptualize a theory of power based on Gramsci's (1971) notion of hegemony. Hegemony occur when one group of people rule another by manipulating cultural (i.e., beliefs, perceptions, and values) and societal norms that benefit those in power. Even if the original intention of critical theorists was to name the "Other" as a way of challenging the status quo, not to simplify power, it seems that is how it has been used. Feminist and poststructural theories, however, help us see power as more complex and fluid (Gannon & Davies, 2007).

Foucault (1977), a poststructuralist, stated that power is not hierarchical, but capillary. In other words, power proceeds in every direction. Zembylas (2005) believes that power is dispersed, manifested, and exercised in discursive practices. Power is not a possession; it is unstable and localized. To Foucault and many feminists, power is seen as productive, not just as oppressive. Foucault (1977) discusses how power is operationalized in interactions between individuals and institutions. The notion of capillary power is freeing in the sense that it resists the oppressor/oppressed dichotomy. Foucault's notion of power embraces the messiness of relations and interactions, which I appreciate.

My intent is to demonstrate how the students and I negotiated power through interactions. Through our conversations about the teachers on the playground and Parks's life, we discussed the vertical ways power can circulate, while at other times power circulates more horizontally in relationships. It is helpful to view the coercive and collaborative relations of power in classrooms (Wink, 2000). Even if not always explicitly exerted, power among the students and with teachers or other adult figures is always present because of the authority teachers have over students.

CHAPTER 2

Constructing Privilege as a Child
Autoethnography as a Process of Consciousness-Raising

> It is important to view the self as an emergent and changing "project" not a stable and fixed entity. Over time our view of our self changes, and so, therefore, do the stories we tell about ourselves. In this sense, it is useful to view self-definition as an ongoing narrative project. (Goodson, 1998, p. 11)

We all experience stories differently. There is not one right interpretation. We all have stories and images, whether photos or memories, that at some level capture our lives. In this chapter I share several images and stories from my childhood to situate the book in the narratives of my life. As educators it is necessary to bring to consciousness the experiences from our lives that shape the decisions we make and interactions we have with students.

As the opening quote states, we are all emergent and changing projects. The view of our self changes over time, as do the stories we tell about ourselves. Each time I approach the images and stories below, I see something new and different. While I interpret the images and stories in one way at this time, it is by no means the right way, nor does it mean that my interpretation will not change over time. I invite you to read these images and stories alongside your own experiences. I also invite you to ponder experiences and images from your own life.

1. Do you interpret the images the way I did?
2. Are there aspects of the images that I miss or choose not to acknowledge, perhaps because it is too difficult?
3. Who or what is missing or silenced from the images?
4. What are images and/or memories from your own childhood that demonstrate privilege and/or oppression?
5. What stories continue to surface in your memory that shape who you are today?

Figure 2.1. Preschool Photograph at Age 5

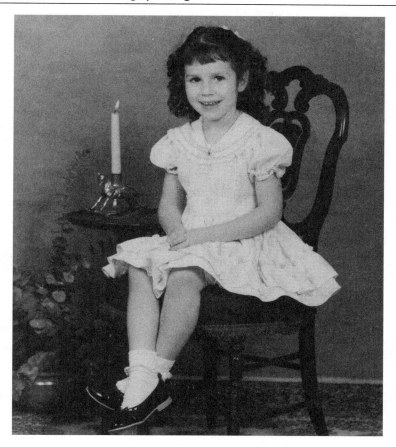

6. What can you learn from your narratives? How do the experiences influence your beliefs that shape teaching and/or researching?

As a 5-year-old (Figure 2.1), I sit perched on a well-crafted wooden chair next to a brass candleholder and on an ornate rug. My eyes are drawn to three things. One is the white frilly socks and black patent-leather shoes I have on my feet. The socks complement the ruffles of the dress and indicate privilege. How many young children have the means to wear a frilly dress and fancy socks and shoes for picture day at their preschool? Other school pictures show me wearing dresses hand-smocked by my mother or grandmother. Second, I notice the curly locks of hair pulled back in white bows. I have vivid memories of my mother tightly rolling strands of hair around

Figure 2.2. Baton Lessons

pink sponge rollers after washing my hair the night before special events, such as picture day. Sleeping on a head of sponge rollers is not easy but was necessary to ensure that the curls would hold throughout the school day. Third, if you look closely I am wearing a gold heart locket necklace. While I do not have a vivid memory of the specifics of this necklace, it perhaps signifies privilege. Not all children have gold lockets to wear around their necks. Although I cannot remember, maybe there was a photo inside the gold heart of someone special. Overall, even to have copies of this picture (and many others) means that my parents had the resources to purchase sets of photos when the proofs were sent home.

Standing with a baton in hand coupled with a trophy, Figure 2.2 is one of many photographs that show me participating in extracurricular activities. At age 9, I had already had several years of baton lessons. My parents spent many hours driving across town each week to transport me to and from classes. The baton twirlers performed in halftime shows at local basketball games and participated in annual parades. My parents were able not only to pay for lessons and equipment but also for the uniforms, such as this sailor suit, for performances. In addition to baton lessons—both group and private—I took dance lessons and gymnastics (both of which prepared

Figure 2.3. Chicago Skyline

me for cheerleading in secondary schools), piano, tennis, and, for a brief period of time, voice lessons. My parents also paid annually for me to attend a sculpture day, which allowed children to create clay sculptures while working with an artist. Twice mine were selected as the winner and placed either in the fountain at the mall or at the public library for display. These extracurricular experiences cost money not only to attend, to pay for gas to shuttle me to and from, and to purchase costumes, but also time on my parents' part to bring me to lessons and events. These experiences gave me opportunities to work with others and establish social knowledge, develop leadership skills, and become a "well-rounded" person—all of which are privileged opportunities and typically expected in order to succeed in school.

Figure 2.3 is an image of the Chicago skyline in 1994, which symbolizes the church trips I went on every summer as a youth. This particular trip was to Chicago, where the youth led vacation Bible school sessions each day, at night sang concerts around the city, and worked with local churches. I have many photographs of me with African American children, many from low-income families, but to protect their identity and to not appropriate their images, even years later, I decided to use this skyline to represent the privilege I had of traveling all over the United States for church trips. Many of the images and memories I have are with marginalized groups such as native Hawaiians, Latino/a children, and African American children. My parents had the means to pay the fees for travel, hotels, and food. I grew up as a member of a large, conservative church in the South that prided itself on taking trips to "save the souls" of lost people. For example, in Phoenix we led daily Bible-school camps for children in a low-income neighborhood with mainly Latino/a families. We spent our days playing games, telling Bible stories, and doing crafts—all related to Jesus. However, we did not engage in practical work with concrete effects of changing systematic issues of poverty and/or racism. I always had an unsettling feeling about sweeping in as the well-off White girl to tell people with less material privilege than myself that Jesus loves them and they should believe the way I was supposed to. Who was I to make such a claim to them?

Figure 2.4 captures the celebration my family had after my mother completed her Ph.D. in early childhood education. As you can see, she pursued this degree not before she had children, but while we were all growing up. She traveled 90 miles one way to go to a university several days a week for classes and a graduate assistantship position. What is not captured in this photo is my father also receiving a doctorate (before the children were born) in religious education administration. Growing up with both parents with doctorates is not all that common and set a precedent. My siblings and I knew that education was valued and expected. My sister and I have both gone on to receive doctorates. All of us have degrees past high school, which positions us, even today, in privileged ways not only financially but also socially, seen as experts in our communities.

MY HISTORIES

As the previous images and narratives describe, my childhood in the southern United States, or the "Deep South," allowed me to grow into a certain position of power and privilege that I have examined critically only over the past 10 years. Before then, while I might have had uneasy feelings or chose to suppress questions about race, class, and privilege, I did not intentionally or consciously look at how my experiences in life as a White, middle-class, heterosexual female with no disabilities raised in a conservative Christian home shaped my beliefs and worldviews. I did not think critically about how this upbringing directly influenced my teaching philosophy and practices in the classroom. As educators, we all need to intentionally call into question our life experiences—memories, images, stories—that shape the educators we are and continue to be as our life stories evolve. This book is an attempt to be explicit about the implicit. Our day-to-day activities and relationships are not always examined for aspects of power, position, and privilege—these are implicit parts of who we are. Through writing and viewing images of childhood experiences juxtaposed with teaching interac-

Figure 2.4. Mother's Ph.D. Graduation Celebration

tions, I make explicit how teaching is connected to who we are as people—our beliefs, families, childhood experiences, and relationships.

My childhood years encompassed the 1980s and 1990s. After high school I moved to an urban university to pursue a degree in early childhood education. During my first years of teaching, I went back to school for a master's degree in early childhood education. I had teaching experiences in an urban school, suburban schools, and abroad in Japanese preschools. After returning to the United States, I completed a doctoral program in literacy, culture, and language education. Currently, I teach and research at a Midwestern university.

Family

My nuclear family is made up of a mother, father, older sister, and younger brother. My parents waited, intentionally, 10 years after marrying before having children. Up until I graduated from high school, my father served as a Baptist minister in various capacities (minister of music, youth, and education). My mother, who had worked as a reading teacher, stayed home and raised three children. Once all three of the children were in school, she went back to college and eventually earned a Ph.D. I remember hearing my mother describe how there were some people in our church who disagreed with her choice to drive a long distance to pursue a Ph.D. Some of them may have thought a woman's role was to be submissive to the husband, in the most traditional way, and stay at home with the children. Ironically, my mother's absence a couple of days each week allowed me to develop independence and traditionally gendered skills in cooking, ironing, cleaning, and caring for my siblings.

My parents' worldviews were not only shaped by their schooling experiences, but by their hometown: both were raised in New Orleans, a city with a long history of negative race relations and economically segregated neighborhoods. As a family we traveled to New Orleans about twice a year to visit extended family. My family experience was (and still is) a weaving of forward-thinking educational ideas and conservative religious values. I received messages from both my parents to be a strong, independent woman. My parents encouraged me to pursue multiple degrees, to find equal respect and shared values in a romantic partner, and to be able to financially support myself.

Church

My family was at church every time the doors opened—Sunday morning and evening, Wednesday night for a meal and prayer meeting, and for any other special event. This was nonnegotiable. As a minister's daughter, people noticed when you were not there and even asked about your absence when you returned. This was made evident one Easter as a young elementary student, when I woke up sick. As my father and mother both had responsibilities at church and I was too young to stay at home alone, I was dressed in a frilly dress and brought to church. Too sick to interact with other people, they laid a plastic blue and red rest mat on the floor of my father's office and gave me some crackers and apple juice to snack on if needed. There I lay as my parents fulfilled their roles.

The church congregants were White and primarily families with middle- to upper-class economic status. I have memories of sitting in classes as a middle and high school student and wrestling with concepts being taught about Christianity, especially the role of women. There was an exclusivity message sent through the literal readings and interpretations of the Bible. Religious doctrine was bloody. Not literally, but in the sense that the dominant discourses in teachings and songs were about Jesus dying on a cross. The main theme I heard over and over again was accepting Jesus and being baptized in order to save my soul from going to hell. This was the one and only way to heaven. There was a common understanding that my purpose in life was to witness or proselytize the Good News (i.e., salvation from Jesus). A doctrine of men being the head of the church and households was lived out. The pastor was always a White man. Women only served in the role of preschool or children's ministries director (my mom served as the preschool director). While I enjoyed the friendships and stability that church offered, I wonder how a religion based on exclusivity shaped my beliefs.

School

I attended a citywide magnet school for elementary school that was housed in two separate buildings (grades K–2 in one building and K, 3–5 in another—the kindergarten students in both buildings were neighborhood children), where attendance was determined by a recommendation from a teacher based on leadership capabilities and academics. My kindergarten teacher recommended me (she thought I would be a teacher one day—she nailed that). For grades 6 through 12, I attended the school I was zoned for based on my address. While the elementary school experience was more homogenous in that there were mostly Caucasian students from mainly affluent families, my secondary years were different. All students in the school district attended one of two high schools (grades 9 to 12). I do not remember having many teachers who were not Caucasian—only one 6th-grade history teacher and one 8th-grade English teacher. In fact, I cannot remember ever having a person of another race at my home. All birthday parties were comprised of Caucasian children. All the guests my parents had over, usually related to church, were Caucasian. All the neighborhood children we played with were Caucasian.

In high school, my perception was that the community frowned on interracial dating, and although we all took the same classes, students socially self-segregated along racial and economic lines, and did not normally hang out together on the weekends with students of other races or economic levels. For example, in the lunchroom students self-segregated by the tables they sat at. The clothes worn were also an indicator of who students associated with. For example, words such as "preppy," "nerdy," "skater," and "gangster" were phrases to label groups of people. In my advanced placement and honors classes, I do not remember having many African American peers, although there were numerous Asian and Indian American students. This feeds the typical stereotype of Asian students being smart while African Americans and Latino/a Americans are in grade-level or remedial classes.

Teaching

After attending a 4-year university in an urban city center, I graduated as an early childhood teacher. I taught in urban and suburban elementary schools in the United States and preschools in Japan. My first job was teaching kindergarten in a low-income, urban school with a primarily African American student body. A few vivid memories from that first year include a boy who acted out sex on the floor of our classroom and around poles in the lunchroom numerous times. I did not know how to respond to these outbursts. How do you talk with a parent about this? I had another male student who moved from place to place in full motion, by turning cartwheels, and he knocked over bookshelves or hit lockers with his feet several times. When I communicated about his behavior to his mother, she decided to come to the school, unannounced, and whip him with her belt in front of the class. How is a first-year teacher to respond to this? While this description might perpetuate a stereotype, my intention in sharing it is to show the complexity of relationships in schools and the necessity of teachers to examine their own beliefs. Many times incidences such as this uncover deep, hidden ideologies—as it did for me even years later. Was my belief of not using corporal punishment a better way to discipline? Who was I to judge this parent's way of handling her child's behavior just because it was different from my ideas?

The following few years I taught in a suburban school district near the downtown district I first taught in. Why did I yearn to move? Perhaps because I felt like an outsider in a school that had mainly African American students and faculty. Perhaps because I did not know how to relate to families and children whom I perceived as different from my own. Perhaps because I did not agree with the curriculum materials I was expected to teach with. Moving to a well-funded district of relatively affluent families did not mean that difficulties went away. During my second year of teaching, I remember hearing conversations among parents and faculty about the influx of inner-city children attending the school after apartments were designated as government housing. The dynamics of the neighborhood school changed. Conversations circulated around increased behavioral issues and lowering test scores. To solve this perceived problem, parents worked together with city officials and rezoned the apartment complex as business property, leveling the apartment complex. Families were displaced. Several students' families' in my class had to look for a new place to live, and the children knew they would not return to the school in the fall. I witnessed the power, position, and privilege that I lived among. The affluent White families and faculty were not comfortable with the changing makeup of the school population and did something about it.

EXPERIENCES OF OTHERING

The context of my upbringing led me to internalize Othering, even though I am uncomfortable with it. While I did not realize the Othering I was doing in the narratives shared previously and throughout the book, it was the case. I positioned myself as better than Others: my experiences, my language, my dress, my beliefs on parenting, my behaviors, and my teaching styles were better at some level. This is difficult to acknowledge. But understanding that difference is not a deficit or a negative is hard to process. The stories in this section illustrate the Othering I constructed growing up and while teaching.

* * *

To get to our church, we had a few choices of routes. One was to take a highway that circled the outside of the city. The other was to take a variety of paths through the city. My mother preferred the route around the city, possibly because there were fewer stoplights and it seemed faster. My father usually drove through the city and often through the primarily African American, lower-income section of town. I would sit in the backseat and peer outside the window. These neighborhoods looked so different from mine and the neighborhood borders were clear. The houses were smaller, older, and did not look as well-kept as the ones in my neighborhood. As we began to drive through these other neighborhoods to church, I would lock my door, or at least check it each time. Why did I feel the need to lock my door? Where did this fear come from?

* * *

As previously mentioned, one student in my kindergarten class, Dontrell, was very active. He would do cartwheels up and down the hallway, knocking over bookshelves with his feet. He also had one of the most beautiful smiles, which could light up a room, and he would often charm me, peering up at me with his chocolate eyes and pearly whites. As a new teacher, I was not sure how to work with him on controlling his body in ways that would be safe not only for him, but also for other students, while not crushing his spirit. As a novice teacher, I quickly learned that communicating with parents about "misbehavior" was not always a good decision for me (or perhaps for the student) because parents might respond to the child in a way that I believed to be inappropriate. My beliefs on discipline align with the word's etymology, which means "to guide." I do not see corporal punishment or spanking as the most appropriate way to discipline a child.

After sending a note home to Dontrell's mother about his behavior, she showed up unannounced. Dressed in her work uniform (a security guard), she pulled the leather belt off her waist and began to beat him in front of the class. I froze. He flopped like a fish out of water on the carpeted floor as we all sat and watched. So many thoughts crossed my mind in a flash. I remember thinking, is this really happening? Do I jump in, risk getting hit, and pull her child away from her? Do I ask her to step out in the hall and talk with me? Do I send for help from the principal or counselor? Do I raise my voice at her, demanding she stop? While I had learned in education classes to respect different ways of parenting, I was not prepared for this parent's response to the notes I sent home. Why did she feel the need to reprimand him in front of his peers and me? How did my position as a young White teacher influence how she responded to the letters I sent home? The whipping ended before I could utter a word. The details of what happened next are hard for me to remember, but what sticks out in my memory is the action between mother and son and how I felt frozen, unsure how to respond. I do not remember exactly what I said to her or Dontrell when it concluded. I do remember trying to comfort him when she left the room. I made a decision to not send home a note again about his active nature. I was too afraid of what might occur at home if what I witnessed happened in front of a room of 20 people in a public space. I share this memory, not to perpetuate stereotypes but as an example of how I struggled in my Whiteness and naivete as a 1st-year teacher, unsure of how to respond to parenting styles different from what I experienced. This was a pivotal moment of Othering that I continue to analyze critically.

*   *   *

These vignettes are only an overview of significant moments I remember from my childhood and first years of teaching, all of which influence the person I am today. Additional vignettes are shared throughout the book paired with teaching encounters I had with children. I do not share these as a way to point a finger at those I love and/or who had key relationships with me as a child. Nor do I share vignettes of Othering as a way to reinscribe racism, classism, and White privilege. I share these as moments of consciousness-raising, which as an adult I have unpacked, from a critical standpoint, drawing on Whiteness theory and other critical and feminist perspectives.

While many of the episodes could be read as patronizing Others, my intent is to share, as honestly as possible, the way I felt in the moment and how I now have uncovered deep-seated beliefs. It is a process. A changing process. Autoethnography allows educators to examine life histories, however difficult; in hopes of social action—social changes in the way one teaches and lives their life.

CHAPTER 3

Students as Co-Inquirers
Our Critical Literacy Inquiry

> For much of conventional educational research, context is a static entity and the researcher an observer of the context who employs methods to focus on something discrete. As teacher researchers, we recognize how we are implicated in actively shaping the various, at times conflicting, contexts in our professional lives. (Campano, 2007, p. 117)

As I entered the classroom, which would become our learning community for the summer, I observed plastic coverings over the materials and counters. As a university summer program, the location rotated each year to a different elementary school. As temporary teachers in the summer, we were required to bring our own materials and not disturb the school's resources. I immediately began to visualize how I could move furniture around and create an inviting space among the large plastic sheets covering cabinets. A small group of teachers met together at a round table in a common space. This was my first introduction to the other teachers of the program, as they came from various schools and districts across the area. After a brief meeting about logistics, I strolled back to my room anxious to begin the transformation. I brought in my own books, math manipulatives and games, watercolors, art materials, blocks, and puzzles. To brighten the room, I put solid-colored paper on bulletin boards, knowing the students' art and writing would soon cover them.

CONTEXTUALIZING SPACES AND FACES:
THE PROGRAM SITE AND CHILDREN

As stated in the opening quote for this chapter, Campano (2007) writes that context is seen as a static entity in much educational research. Campano's notion of teacher researchers shaping the contexts as much as their students resonates with me, and it is also echoed by Fecho and Meacham (2007), who argue "all actors in a context are shaped by that context, but also shape that context" (p. 168). This implies that each learning community is unique. Even though the description of my teaching context might sound similar to other places and connect with teachers (I hope it does), it had its own distinctive histories and cultures, shaped by the city, school, and program, as well as by the beliefs of each child and adult in the space.

The Program

I had taught in this summer program for several years when previously living in the South. As a classroom teacher, after earning my master's degree, I taught in the program. When I learned that I would be back living in this city for one summer during my graduate studies, I inquired about teaching in this program again. There was a position available to teach students, most of whom had just finished kindergarten (two students began kindergarten the following autumn). I gladly accepted the opportunity to learn alongside children again as a teacher.

During my graduate coursework, I had read many texts on critical literacy and was curious to explore it with children. Therefore, I approached this teaching opportunity as a teacher researcher (Cochran-Smith & Lytle, 1993, 2009), using the experience to explore some of the questions I had about critical literacy in early childhood. I decided to collect data through videotaping and audio-recording classroom interactions, capturing student learning with photographs and artifacts (drawings and writing), and writing field notes and daily reflections.

The university-sponsored enrichment program was a 6-week, half-day program. Children who had completed kindergarten through 5th grade learned through "hands-on/minds-on" experiences (i.e., not scripted programs). My responsibility was to provide learning experiences in reading, writing, math, arts, and inquiry in science and social studies. The students left my classroom 1 hour a day for music, art, library, or science, which rotated on a weekly basis. I acknowledge that the summer program differed from what happens in a regular school year. There were no grades or pressures of standardized testing that many teachers feel. However, the program did take place in a school building, and children participated in school-like activities such as reading and writing workshops, math games, and science experiments.

Because of my interest in critical literacy, I sent parent questionnaires (see Appendix A) home to families to get a better idea of how children talk about social injustices outside of school (or if they do not talk about them at all). While I did not have the opportunity to visit the children's homes or observe students in environments outside of the program, the parental questionnaire gave me a small window into students' lives beyond school activities, who they spent time with, and the ways in which they discussed (or did not) injustices with their families.

I also wrote weekly newsletters (see Appendix B for an example), which shared with families the topics and inquiry questions we explored. The newsletters explained the books we read and the focus of writing activities, math games, and other learning engagements. I listed the children's books we read (related to Rosa Parks and segregation), and the children were allowed to "check out" these books each day to read at home. Only one parent (a Caucasian mother) approached me with inquiries about teaching children about segregation. She was actually grateful, because what happened during the day prompted questions at home, which gave her space to talk with her son about segregation.

The mixture of additional adults was also an important aspect of our classroom environment. Throughout the summer, I had three teaching aides who typically rotated on a weekly basis. Two of them were newly certified teachers awaiting their first classroom teaching positions. The other, who was with us toward the end of the summer, had many years of experience. There were high expectations from parents that the program would serve as a place of individualized instruction, especially in relation to reading and writing. An obvious advantage of having an extra adult in the room is to facilitate small-group instruction and help with teaching. However, I was not always sure the aide agreed or even understood my pedagogical beliefs and decisions to engage young children in critical dialogue.

In addition to these aides, the program served as a practicum site for master's-level university students. On many days there were a handful of university students in the classroom to observe and teach. In addition to teaching aides and university students, there were also student volunteers, who were teenage children of other program employees. While I appreciated all these extra hands, at times I felt that there were too many; sometimes it seemed there were more adults than children!

The Children: My Co-Inquirers

Previously, I had taught for several years in the school district where the summer program took place and had lived in the community for almost a decade. Therefore, I had prior experiences to help me understand the general cultures and contexts of my students' lives. At the heart of this Southern city is a past of struggle with civil rights and overt prejudices. An ingrained assumption is that religion, especially conservative evangelical interpretations of Christianity, is the ideology that governs interactions, morality, and laws. The school district is physically "over the mountain" from the downtown, urban center, and is made up largely of upper-middle-class

TABLE 3.1. Gender and Racial Categories as Provided by Parents

	Asian	African American	Caucasian	More Than One Race	Total
Females	0	2	4	2*	8
Males	1	3	9	0	13

*Two girls (Annie and Ellie), a set of twins, were identified by their parent(s) as Caucasian and Asian. To manage potential conflicts of interest as the classroom teacher, I did not have access to the parental questionnaires until after the summer program ended, so I was unaware of this biracial identification. Based on skin tone, I identified these girls as "White" in conversations with them.

TABLE 3.2. Income Categories of Children

Income Category	Number of Students
$0–50,000	1 (This child had a history of living with his maternal grandparents; this figure does not reflect the income of both working grandparents.)
$51,000–100,000	8
$101,000–150,000	2
$151,000–175,000	3
$176,000–200,000	2
$201,000 and above	5

families. Suburban school districts such as this one are known as "over-the-mountain" schools, which carry a connotation of being wealthier areas. The district is known for hiring teachers with more progressive teaching philosophies. Through sales tax from malls and higher property taxes, the district is able to support a range of extracurricular activities and invests money in buildings and technologies.

By the nature of parents having to pay weekly fees for the program, and by being marketed as an enrichment program, the trend was for more affluent, Caucasian American families to send their children. Twenty-one out of twenty-seven students returned a parental questionnaire with consent to be in the research study (Tables 3.1 and 3.2). From this questionnaire, 13 identified as male and 8 identified as female. Most students were middle- to upper-class, with only one student living in a household that made less than $50,000 annually (although he lived with his maternal grandparents, who both had middle-class jobs and salaries that would raise this figure). Of the remaining 20 students, 10 had a household income above $151,000. Most students (13) identified as Caucasian. Five children identified as African American and one identified as Asian. There was one set of twins who identified as Caucasian and Asian. While most of the students spent multiple,

FIGURE 3.1. Who Are We?

consecutive weeks in the program, there was a constant flux of classroom dynamics because children were only required to attend a minimum of 3 out of the 6 weeks. Sometimes the 3 weeks were spread out sporadically due to family vacations and summer camps.

CURRICULUM OVERVIEW

It was important to begin building a community atmosphere from day one. Knowing we would only have 6 weeks together, I began from the first day purposefully creating learning engagements for us to get to know one another and as a way for me to observe student interactions for possible ideas for critical literacy inquiries. On the first day, students partnered up and interviewed each other, finding out about families, favorite foods, games, books, and so on. Students used a combination of drawing and writing to record what they learned. On the second day students drew self-portraits. On the third day, students introduced the peer they interviewed and we displayed the portraits and interview notes on a large bulletin board (Figure 3.1).

On the first Thursday and Friday, we read the book *I Went Walking* (Williams, 1992) as a springboard to create a big book (an enlarged text, typically with rhyme, rhythm, and/or repetition of words for emerging readers) about what we saw when walking in and outside of our building. This allowed students to get to know the school and people that they would interact with over the summer. These get-to-know-you experiences were com-

FIGURE 3.2. Playground

plemented with math games, shared reading experiences with big books and songs, shared writing interactions (e.g., Daily News, a writing experience where children share events from their lives), daily recess and snack time outside, and read-alouds of poetry and picture books.

The Playground Bench Incident:
Impetus for Our Critical Literacy Inquiry

Within the first week of our time together I witnessed a situation on the playground that made some of the children and me uncomfortable. The critical literacy inquiry the class explored came from multiple discussions about the recurring events of Mrs. Adams and other teachers telling the students to not sit on the playground bench when eating snacks during recess. One can imagine the heat and humidity of the South. As we entered an empty playground each day, my students searched for a spot of shade to sit under while eating and resting from play (Figure 3.2).

As other classes came outside, teachers would yell at my students, stating that the bench was for adults only. I sat and watched in a state of disbelief and was uncomfortable with how I might respond to these demands. As this was a summer program, I did not have a history of working with any of the teachers. I was not aware of a rule that only adults can sit on benches. This event reminded me of what Rosa Parks might have felt when she was told to move from her seat on the bus. In sharing this with the children, their questions helped to guide our explorations. Table 3.3 summarizes the path

TABLE 3.3. Overview of Critical Literacy Inquiry

Week	Path of the Critical Literacy Inquiry
1	• We spent this week getting to know one another. The students interviewed each other, drawing/writing their responses; they introduced themselves through self-portraits.
	• I spent time listening to students interact, looking for possible springboards for the critical literacy inquiry.
2	• I brought to the class's attention an incident I noticed on the playground—students were told to get up and relocate with their snack during recess. Teachers told them that benches were for adults only. We discussed how we felt and created a class chart of the ways we could respond in the future.
	• I connected the playground incident to Rosa Parks. We read a biography (Schaefer, 2000) about her; I brought in timelines and additional online research about her based on student questions. We did not have access to use the computers in our classroom due to rules of the hosting school district. Therefore, students could not use the Internet while at the summer program to research.
	• The children connected Rosa Parks to Martin Luther King Jr. on their own.
	• One student, Annie, specifically asked me (one-on-one) why White people would create laws to segregate African Americans. She wanted to ask the class to help her answer this question.
	• We began a class audit trail as a way to capture our explorations and guide inquiry.
3	• Because of student questions about segregation, we read *Richard Wright and the Library Card* (Miller & Christie, 1999), *Sister Anne's Hands* (Lorbiecki, 2000), and *The Other Side* (Woodson, 2001).
	• We used a chart to record our thinking about the following questions for each book: What happened? Was it unfair? Why did it happen? What could have been done differently?
	• We continued to add our thinking to the audit trail.
4	• I read *Voices in the Park* (Browne, 2001) to the children. We used the structure of the text to author/illustrate our own class book, *Voices on the Bus*, as a way to understand the multiple perspectives on the bus with Rosa Parks. We spent several days in small groups authoring perspectives (Rosa, the bus driver, other Whites, and other African Americans) and illustrating the pages. We continued to add our thinking to the audit trail.

Continued

TABLE 3.3. Overview of Critical Literacy Inquiry, Continued

Week	Path of the Critical Literacy Inquiry
5	• We read our book, *Voices on the Bus*, together multiple times. • I shared another book about Rosa Parks (Adler, 1995), indicating that she was told to get up on a bus 10 years before the famous arrest, by the same bus driver. We discussed how her decision, supported by a movement of people, to not move the second time was planned and purposeful because they wanted the law changed. • To explore the question "Does it still happen today?," we created a timeline to look at segregation historically. We read *Henry's Freedom Box* (Levine, 2007) for a historical perspective. • Children were interested in where slaves came from; we used a wall-size world map to discuss how slaves and Caucasian people came to America. Questions surfaced: Who was in the United States first? What about Native Americans? • We continued to add our thinking to the audit trail.
6	• We read the book *This Is the Dream* (Shore & Ransome, 2005), which a student found in our class library. We used a quote by Martin Luther King Jr. about resisting through nonviolence as a point of our discussions. There were many connections to previous conversations, books, and people. The author's note in the book states that injustices still happen today; we discussed whether we believed this to be true. • We read the book *Say Something* (Moss, 2008) as a way to discuss injustices that happen in the lives of children at schools. • The children thought of injustices that had happened to them. They illustrated these events through painting and thought of ways to peacefully respond to the situation if it happened again. • We circled back to the incident on the playground and continued to add our thinking to the audit trail.

of our critical literacy inquiry related to discussions around the incident on our playground and Rosa Parks. We used an audit trail as a way to document our learning (Harste & Vasquez, 1998; Vasquez, 2004). An audit trail is a visual display that chronicles the life of an inquiry. Our audit trail, on one large wall, had charts from class discussions, photocopies of book covers, responses to books and incidents, a timeline, notes from small-group discussions used to write our book, *Voices on the Bus*, and other artifacts from our inquiry (Figure 3.3). Table 3.3 is an overview of the critical literacy inquiry for each week of the summer program. This table does not include the curriculum during math or the special classes students attended (i.e., science, music, art, or library).

FIGURE 3.3. Audit Trail

As indicated in Table 3.3, texts are an important part of a critical literacy inquiry in order to expose students to various perspectives on issues. Books are best used as supporting tools when a teacher negotiates with students a path of inquiry. Other types of texts, such as research printed off the Internet as seen in Table 3.3, information gathered through dialogue with other people, and role-play also served as tools for our investigation.

Questioning Critical Inquiry Choices

The incident on the playground bench was difficult for me to witness. Based on the facial expressions I observed as the students were told to move, I felt it was necessary to at least open space for a conversation. Because critical inquiries are lived and come from the lives of those involved, I shared my observations with the students. However, the decision to have a conversation with them was not easy. Was I imposing this inquiry on them? Was it more my curiosity than theirs? Was it my own struggle?

In conversation about the students being told where they could and could not sit, I made a connection to Rosa Parks. Although I realize the connection to Rosa Parks might be viewed as homogenizing and minimizing the struggle of civil rights for African Americans, to do so was not my intention. In part, that tension is a purpose of this book: to reflectively cast a critical perspective on teaching decisions as I was (and continue to) unlearning my Whiteness, position, and privilege in society. Educators encourage teachers to use children's literature and history as entry points into critical literacy conversations (Evans, 2007; Jones, 2006; Lewison, Leland, & Harste,

2007), so I thought discussing the inequality and power relations in Parks's life might open a space for us to discuss what happened on the playground, to nuance how the situations are different, yet both about power.

Reflecting on my decision to connect the playground bench to Parks remains a point of tension. While I now see how the connection could be viewed as inappropriate, I also contemplate how educators might use historical events as examples for young children to process injustices while not reducing the complexity of the events. I wonder how else I might have given my students an entry into a conversation about adult/child power relationships. If we wait for children to experience inequities, either by being the targets of oppression or by being the privileged in power, we may be too late to help students prepare to respond in just ways. The idea behind introducing Rosa Parks into our discussion about the bench was to engender sensitivity to such matters at the place where students best identify with traditionally marginalized people. So I made the connection to Parks, assuming that because of the close geography, local history, and resources in the community (a civil rights museum nearby), the children would have some knowledge of her arrest.

I did not envision the summer inquiry to be an exploration primarily about racism, specifically Jim Crow–era racism. However, because of the students' inquiries after I made a connection to Parks, we followed that direction. This path also resulted in spending that summer (and years since) wrestling with my Whiteness, and, in turn, I presume some of the children might have as well.

Other Possible Avenues for Critical Literacy Inquiry

As the teacher I chose to open space for conversation around what I witnessed on our playground and in relation to Parks. Our critical literacy inquiry could have looked very different. Below are three additional interpretations and other possible ways I could have opened a line of inquiry with the students in relation to the event on our playground.

One possible reading of the playground incident is that as children my students should have gotten up off the bench to be respectful to their elders. Especially in Southern culture, respecting adults through words and actions is generally taught to children at a young age. For example, many children are trained to say, "Yes ma'am" and "No sir" when addressing an adult. In my teaching experience, parents even corrected their children in front of me if I did not insist that they address me with "yes/no ma'am," which made me feel uncomfortable. So one could read what happened on the playground as an adult, Mrs. Adams, reminding students to offer their seats for adults. In this case, the inquiry for the summer could have been to research ways children show respect to adults. However, based on the tone and demeanor of the teachers who demanded my students get off the bench and in response to my own uncomfortable feelings as I witnessed the interaction, I did not feel that going in this direction was truly reflective of what happened. I felt that the situation was more about vertical power and who was in control rather than about respect.

Another possible line of inquiry stemming from the incident could have been to pursue more general questions related to injustices. "Who decides what is an injustice?," "How do we know when we've experienced an injustice?," and "Do we all experience the same injustices?" This line of inquiry would have expanded our research beyond Parks and possibly encouraged children to think of injustices in their own lives and communities in a way that learning about Parks did not.

A third possible line of inquiry could have been to explore what counts as segregation. We talked about how Parks was segregated on the bus, and about racial segregation in relation to restaurants, water fountains, and libraries before laws were changed in the 1960s. In this way, segregation was always cast in a negative light during our discussions. However, we did not explore if there are any positive aspects or other types of "segregation." For example, adults who attend support groups for recovery purposes or children who are pulled out of classrooms for special services at schools are segregated from others. Are these examples of "good" segregation? We could have explored questions such as: "What counts as segregation?," "What are some positive and negative aspects of segregation?," or "What determines if segregation is good or bad?"

In the moment, I chose the path of connecting what happened to us on the playground to Parks. I acknowledge that this was only one way to take up our experience on the playground and that there were many other ways I could have responded. The focus of our conversations about the playground and bus segregation was on control and vertical power (i.e., adult over a child). Who is in power? Who is being controlled? In what ways? Who is advantaged or disadvantaged by such rules?

I also acknowledge that the experience on the playground bench was not the only inequity I observed, as I heard students talk about other instances in their lives. However, this experience seemed to affect many students in my class, and therefore I felt it warranted a conversation at the least, if not potential action.

WRESTLING WITH CRITICAL LITERACY TEACHING

As discussed previously, I struggled in the process of becoming a critical literacy teacher. This was not because I did not believe that children could or even should discuss social injustices, but because of my own developmental beliefs of what is appropriate for young children. Reading texts about teaching from a critical literacy stance and my teaching experiences, however, raised inquiries.

I still question what critical literacy really is, as most scholars do not give a fixed definition. While I understand the desire to not box in critical literacy with a definition, I contemplate questions such as:

1. What does "critical" mean? Does it mean "to agree with me"?
2. What does critical literacy really look like in lived practice?
3. Do we just want children to agree with what *we* think is critical and just?
4. Who are the children trying to please with their criticality?
5. Are we imposing our power as teachers on children?
6. Am I truly critical in my daily interactions? Am I living out critical literacy in all aspects of my life?

While critical theory and its application to pedagogy and literacies might be appealing to some, it has not gone without criticism (Ellsworth, 1989, 1992; Kramer-Dahl, 1996). For example, can dialogue as Freire describes it really happen in educational contexts? Dialogue is difficult because the very nature of the relationships is based on power and identities of sex, race, and class, which are still unjust in our society (Ellsworth, 1989). Sometimes children are left with guilt and fear in a critical curriculum as they deconstruct power relationships, especially if opportunities for reconstruction and social change are not provided. The teacher's role in critical pedagogy could also be viewed as dogmatic. However, teachers like Vasquez (2004) view their role as opening up a variety of possible ways of thinking to their students, not demanding that students agree with their views. I understand that we do not live in a just society, but is that a reason for not trying to have dialogic interactions? How will change ever happen if we do not begin somewhere?

Wink (2000) talks about dialectic in critical literacy as the tension of going back and forth in thoughts, beliefs, and values while learning: "As we learn while teaching and teach while learning, we are in a dialectical process" (p. 47). As teachers, this constant process of reflecting is crucial to hear what our students need and see how our decisions as educators shape their learning (and our own). As educators, we need to continually push our thinking to examine dogmatic practices. What is the catalyst for critical literacy inquiries with our students? What is our motivation for engaging in critical literacy inquiries?

Part II

MOMENTS OF CONSCIOUSNESS-RAISING

CHAPTER 4

Witnessing

What Do You Do with
What You See and Know?

In this chapter, I explore the tensions of witnessing what happened when teachers told my students to get off the playground bench as well as the tensions and lessons from experiences I witnessed related to social injustices earlier in my life. What does someone do with what they see, experience, and know? At times while teaching, I wished I had not observed how my students were treated on the playground. But once I did see, I felt I had to do something.

Witnessing is a term I heard growing up in a Baptist church. I understood this to mean a person sharing about their faith journey. I felt uncomfortable with this concept the way it was described because it came across as being pushy, forced conversations with people whose souls I was supposed to help save. Witnessing is also a term that postcolonial and feminist scholars use to describe marginalized people seeing and/or experiencing, protesting, and organizing against oppressive structures and people. This view of witnessing aligns closer with how I conceptualize it in critical literacy. I see the idea of witnessing as the space where one realizes they are observing and/or experiencing an injustice or inequitable situation and then decides how to respond.

Sahni (2001) argues that relationships are at the heart of critical literacy, especially for young children. She questions more traditional critical scholars, such as Giroux, who write about the macrostructures that oppress people. Sahni argues that men, not women and children, many times control these macro systems of power. She writes that children appropriate literacy and uses the term *creative literacy* to demonstrate that critical literacy is more about relationships on a micro level for children and how children creatively navigate these relationships. Sahni's writing, focusing on relationships, fits with the idea of witnessing. It is through interactions with people that we witness and then respond (even if it is a decision to suppress and stay quiet).

The purpose of this chapter is to cast a critical eye on my response to watching other teachers tell my students to get off the bench. I question how the critical literacy inquiry unfolded once I brought back observations to the students.

1. Did talking about my observations make students uncomfortable?
2. Is it okay for students to be uncomfortable in a critical literacy inquiry?
3. Was it good for children to know that their teacher struggled with how other adults treated them and that school can be about fostering curricular space for these conversations?

I also cast a critical eye on personal experiences I observed as a child, during my first year teaching, and while living in Japan. How did my ideologies and experiences shape the ways I responded (or chose not to respond) to situations?

FLASHBACKS: PERSONAL NARRATIVES WITH WITNESSING

Each of the following memories are examples of situations I was a part of or witnessed where I felt that power was used in an unequal or manipulative way. As we go about our lives, how do we respond to such situations? As teachers, do we provide curricular spaces in the classroom for children to question what they observe and have critical dialogues? Is it appropriate or reasonable for a teacher to initiate conversations with students about moments of inequity that he/she witnesses? How do our histories, identities, and ideologies related to race, class, religion, gender, and other identities shape how we respond to inequities we experience?

Witnessing Homophobia

In high school I was a member of the cheerleading team. A fellow cheerleader, Tyree, was several years older than me and was killed in a car accident after he graduated. What was pivotal after this tragedy were not only the discussions about his race (African American) and gender, as a cheerleader, but his perceived sexual orientation. My gymnastics coach, who knew Tyree, was a conservative fundamentalist minister who believed strongly that homosexuals would go to hell. I found this disturbing and difficult to understand. It made me very uncomfortable because Tyree was one of the most determined, talented, and joyous people I knew. On one occasion when the gymnastics coach attempted to convince me, or explain to me, why Tyree was not in heaven, he was in my face with his hands on my shoulders. And yet it did not fit or work for me. How was I supposed to process and respond to his exclusive views, literally as weights on my shoulders? I viewed this coach as a role model who supported me in gymnastics. I felt conflicted. I remember talking with my mother about the disequilibrium I felt and her comforting me. While I do not remember what she said, it was her presence and lack of judgment that gave me permission to consider that my coach's perspective did not have to be mine. I have finally come to peace about where I think Tyree's soul is, but it has taken years of working through messages I was sent as a child. What is a child to do with what they observe—if what they witness and experience is a common belief or way of being in their community—even if at gut level something does not feel right? I experienced church and Christianity as a way to save the souls of those not like myself. How did these messages shape my beliefs?

Witnessing Proselytizing

After teaching for several years in the United States, I had the opportunity to teach in four preschools in Japan for a year. For many reasons, this was one of the most pivotal years of my life in coming to understand who I am as a person, why I believe what I do, and what I want to do with my life. Alone in a country where I did not speak the language or know many people, I sought out opportunities in the first few months that were similar to what I knew in the United States. Growing up as a Southern Baptist girl, I searched for a church in Japan as a way to get to know people and find some other Westerners to build relationships with while there. I tried out a few churches and my experiences in each of them did not sit well with me. One in particular was a church, mainly of Japanese citizens, that was organizing English lessons for other Japanese people. Although I do not disagree with the idea of organizations, such as churches, offering language lessons, I did not agree with the way this particular group went about it. They wanted me to help teach English lessons, but the catch was that I had to use the Bible to do so. Similarly, one American I met, also living in Japan, asked me if I was going to learn Japanese. When I told her I was learning some basic conversation phrases, she responded that she was trying to become fluent so she could convert Japanese people to Christianity. These experiences felt manipulative. Offering free English lessons but using only the Bible as the text seemed like an unequal use of power. I felt conflicted: Should I teach English lessons with the Bible to maintain relationships with people while living in a country where I did not know many people, or should I walk away? I struggled with the idea of continuing to attend a church that did not see this use of power as problematic, and eventually decided I could not participate in this type of exclusivity. I learned that I do not have to participate in inequities I witness. However, I did not speak up and voice why I quit attending the church. A combination of feeling uncomfortable with what I witnessed and the language barrier contributed to my silence.

WHO IS RESPONSIBLE FOR ACTING ON WHAT THEY WITNESS?

While teaching in the summer program, I knew I wanted to approach inquiry from a critical literacy stance. I also knew I wanted the inquiry to come from the lives of the children, so I spent time getting to know them and observing what they did and talked about to one another. I did not expect an event, like the one on the playground, to happen. But as I watched the teachers yelling to my students from the school door that they could not sit on the bench, I knew I could not ignore my feelings. While I understood that the teachers wanted a spot in the shade to sit during recess, I also felt that the children had a right to the shade. How could we all rest in the comfort of the large tree's branches as a respite from the heat and humidity?

Reactions to Sharing What I Witnessed

What to do? That was the question I contemplated for the remainder of the day and evening. Would I bring up with the children what I saw or just let it go and comply with the teachers' requests? As my reflective teaching notes indicate (recorded in an audio journal), I decided at least to bring up my observations to the students and see where they might go with the topic:

> Today I decided to bring up to the class the issue I noticed on the playground when the children, who came outside before everyone else and sat on the bench in the shade to eat their snacks, were asked to move by the other teachers when [they] came out. I just wanted to see how or what the children thought about it—if they thought it was fair or not. . . . One girl made an interesting comment: "That's just the way it is; that they're adults so you move." I'm just not really sure where to go with it next. I feel like I've prompted and prodded with several questions and I could not get them to grasp what I was hoping they would. I'm not sure if I should go back tonight and watch the video tape again and maybe have a couple of questions or comments tomorrow of what we can do [in response to the teachers' requests]. Also, I guess because the teachers who asked them to move are not here this week, so [the requests] didn't happen again on the playground today, I'm not sure whether to exhaust this or maybe try it one more day and

see what happens . . . Not sure if I should bring a book or read a book that talks about other people having to give up their seats. Maybe I can find a Rosa Parks book and use that as a way to talk with them and get conversation going. I'll just have to think on that a little bit. (Teaching Reflection Note, Tuesday, June 10)

These notes capture the uncertainty I had with deciding how to respond to what I witnessed. Once I brought my observations back to the class, I was a little surprised that the children did not openly talk about what happened. Looking back, why should it have been surprising for me to expect young children to talk with me (a teacher they had only recently met) about the direction another teacher gave them, even if they felt it was unfair? These notes also show how hesitant I was through the language I used, such as "maybe," "I'm not sure," and "I guess." I chose to use a picture book of a historical example as a springboard for conversation. This felt safe in the moment when I was a little uneasy about where conversations might go related to race. Because Rosa Parks was from the same state as these children, I thought they might have some knowledge about her and the bus boycott.

When I examine these teaching decisions using Whiteness theory perspectives (Giroux, 1997; McIntyre, 1997; Sleeter, 1993), I now see how the choice to bring Parks into the conversation about the bench might be viewed as inappropriate. The struggle of African Americans for basic civil rights is not equal to children being asked to not sit on a bench in the shade by teachers. Was I comparing apples to oranges? Two days later, I contemplated if I should continue to create spaces for conversation about the bench issue or just to let it fizzle:

I was thinking this morning that it's a struggle to figure out how much you prod and push children and how much you just let an issue die—if they don't seem to be going with you. After looking at the video from yesterday—the discussions we've had so far about the bench outside on the playground and the discussion about how it reminded me of Rosa Parks having to move her seat on the bus—I think I'll give it just one more try this morning. Some of them had asked if she [Parks] had died yet and I told them I would look on the Internet since the book [I read to them] had been printed before her death. I think I might pose the question one more time—the comparison of her getting up because of her skin color [to their experience on the bench]. [And ask them] if they had to get up because of their age? And see if that pushes the discussion again or if I think that this issue is one that I just need to leave alone. We'll see what happens today. (Teaching Reflection Notes, Thursday, June 12)

After spending a couple days talking with the students about what I witnessed on the playground and introducing Parks to the children by reading a picture-book biography, I found myself uneasy with the progress (or lack thereof) of conversation. The children became interested in Parks's life, asking lots of questions about her and if she was still alive. They seemed more concerned with Parks than with the bench incident, an event that many of them experienced themselves. Why might they choose to ask more questions about something that took place a few decades back and not choose to talk about an experience that happened to them a few days ago? Dealing with what we experience or witness is often more uncomfortable than talking about a historical event that we can distance ourselves from. Why should that have been surprising? If I was having a difficult time deciding to bring up the topic of the bench to the children, should it have been astonishing that they, too, did not feel comfortable with the topic?

Interactions with Mrs. Adams Again

Several weeks later, when Mrs. Adams returned to teaching, the bench incident happened again. Even though we had spent several weeks talking about the bench and more time exploring racial bus segregation, students did not respond the way I had hoped when they were told to move. I wanted them to say something to the teachers about sharing the bench, as there was space for several people to sit on it. Alternately, I hoped they would offer a suggestion about bringing out folding chairs or a blanket to put on the ground under the tree, like we discussed. But none of these ideas came from the children's mouths when they were told to get up. Reflecting on this, I see I had romantic ideas of how a critical literacy inquiry would happen. Having conversations in the classroom is not enough, especially when young children are faced with speaking up to an adult, a teacher, who has more power than them and someone whose class they enjoyed going to periodically. How naïve on my part. These teaching notes capture what I witnessed several weeks later on the playground:

> Today on the playground, I was walking out to the bench under the big tree and I saw Logan sitting there with one other friend. Mrs. Adams started yelling at them as she was walking out. I was a few steps behind her and felt really uncomfortable. I wanted to see their response but at the same time I didn't want to sit down. I just wasn't sure what to do. She said that was a teachers' bench and that they could not sit there. Logan kind of gave this grimace or a look like he was sad but he got up anyway. I'd like to talk with him one-on-one about that and see what his thoughts were.

As I sat down on the bench some other children came and sat with me. There was space. Mrs. Adams was worried about two other teachers across the playground that were sitting in the sun. She commented that she should do something to get them to come sit in the shade but she didn't ever call them over or say anything. She just stayed in the shade and talked on her cell phone. It is really uncomfortable when another teacher(s) doesn't promote what you're doing and it's hard for me to know what to say or do especially in a situation where we are in and out every couple of weeks. It's just difficult when different teachers have different rules. What do you do as a teacher in a situation like this? (Teaching Reflection Notes, Monday, July 7)

Since I did not have a working relationship with other teachers, I struggled with what appeared to be normal rules about the playground. It seemed that there was a list of expectations that I was not privy to, and I felt caught between what I thought was fair for children (and teachers) and what other adults thought. As I walked out to the playground behind Mrs. Adams yelling at Logan and a few other students, I hesitated. Part of me wanted to see how they would respond, a glimmer of hope that they might say something. Part of me was afraid of how to respond. Would the children expect me to speak up for them after I brought my observations from several weeks ago back to them? Was it my responsibility as the adult to speak up for them?

Teaching from a critical literacy stance is hard. When we have conversations with children about injustices we witness, we, too, are held accountable, by the children to practice what we preach, so to speak. They were watching me to see how I would respond. I chose to watch how the students responded, a cowardly choice. They sheepishly packed up their snacks and hobbled off to find another place to eat. I sat down on the bench and over time other students came up to sit by me. The next day, I decided to talk with Logan about what had happened:

It's a really tough situation for him or for children in general, I'm noticing, because he feels like he should be able to sit on the bench too, but [does not want] to be disrespectful to adults. How [do I] help children find their voice to say things and have conversations with adults in a way that lets them express what they're feeling and what they think, and not to just be socialized by these rules of adults [getting the bench]? [This is] really difficult, really tough, and I had to admit to him that I wasn't sure what to say or do. I made a connection to the book *Say Something*, where [the main character] hoped that other friends at the lunch table around her would say something to help her but instead they sat quietly by, which upset her. [It] kind of made me feel a little guilty that I wasn't sure what to say to this teacher when I noticed that Logan was not able to sit in the shade. It's difficult, difficult for me too. (Teaching Reflection Notes, Tuesday, July 8)

After not intervening with Logan on the playground the previous day, I felt I needed to at least talk with him and express how much I, too, was struggling with what to do. Social action, a tenet so often talked about with critical literacy, is not easy when you are one of the players. As Logan told me in another conversation, he thought I should have said something to Mrs. Adams. Agreeably so. Why did I not, as the adult, speak up for what we had been discussing? Going public with our inquiries was harder than I thought it would be. Even though I had read many books and articles about teachers doing critical literacy inquiries with students, many of which had actions in public spaces, I did not quite grasp the ramifications of doing this.

Could I really expect students to approach Mrs. Adams? What are the social identities of student and teacher relationships that were circulating in this situation? How did my bringing observations to the class about the bench position Mrs. Adams? I acknowledge that the students and I never approached Mrs. Adams to let her know our feelings and possible solutions. There are several reasons for this. One, I was scared and unsure how to respond. I had never met Mrs. Adams until the playground incident, and I did not feel safe challenging her request in front of students. Another reason is that teachers only had to teach for 3 out of 6 weeks. I taught all weeks, but Mrs. Adams was only there the first and last two. As the students and I initially explored the bench episode, she was not around for us to approach. Therefore, her voice is not reflected in this book. It is not my intention to silence her, but to share from my perspective what I perceived to happen from an event I witnessed.

Responding to an Experience When Others Are Watching

Bringing my observations back to the class was also risky because I had aides and preservice teachers in my classroom. How did they view my teaching from a critical literacy stance? At times I felt like I was under surveillance. Because the program also served as a practicum site for the university's master's program in teacher education, I had a steady flow of college students in my room. On Thursday mornings, I usually had up to 10 university students. Unfortunately, there was not downtime for me to have in-depth conversations about curricular decisions with the university students.

My teaching reflection journal captured this tension of working among other educators who I could not be sure understood or agreed with my practices:

Yesterday [an aide asked if I had brought up the playground bench incident] because older students had asked my younger students to get off their seats. I told her that it was the teachers who had asked and I talked with her a little bit about it. She connected it to a time when she was a child and a lady broke in line in front of her and her mom, and her mom had wanted her to stick up for herself. I've been dealing with this dilemma of having other adults in the room and am not sure how they feel about me bringing up [the playground bench incident] with the children and if they understand the purpose behind it, or if they see the reason for it. (Teaching Reflection Notes, Friday, June 13)

Feeling under surveillance by university students and not completely sure what the various aides thought about my curricular decisions did provide a sense of uncertainty for me. Another aide worked closely with me in planning and facilitating small-group discussions around the class book we made about Parks; however, she was the only person who seemed to understand and support our critical inquiry.

MOMENTS OF CONSCIOUSNESS-RAISING

We live in communities where inequities happen. What do we do with what we witness, not just as citizens but also as educators? How do our fluid identities and ideologies influence what and how we choose to respond? What do we feel is appropriate to bring back for conversation in classroom spaces? Does fear or the myth that teaching is neutral keep us from talking with young children about social inequities? Do we hold romantic ideals that prompt us to live in an unrealistic space of protecting innocent children? The reality is that young children live in a world where people are not treated humanely and fairly for a variety of reasons. Children experience injustices in their relationships, much like I knew in my gut that the power differential between my gymnastics coach and I was not equal, so I did not know how to respond to his declarations that homosexuals are going to hell. I believed that as a child it was not my place to speak up against the beliefs of an adult whom I admired as a coach. So how could I really expect Logan and other children to voice their beliefs and feelings?

Logan, along with other children and myself, struggled with what we witnessed on the playground. I kept the tensions inside for a day while I decided how I wanted to approach the topic with the students. Even once I shared my observations with the students, I still struggled with how the curriculum unfolded. Logan kept the tensions inside until the end of the summer program, when he painted about his experience and talked with me

(Kuby, 2013c). We all choose different ways to take action on the inequities we witness.

As an adult, it does not necessarily become easier to speak up about injustices you witness even though with age, power relationships and experiences can shift. But I wonder if as a child I had been a part of classrooms where the common discourse and culture was to question unequal power situations and social injustices, would I be different as an adult today? Would I have been able to speak up my first year of teaching when a mother whipped her child in front of his peers? Would I have spoken up to the Japanese church members and other Westerners who used free English lessons as the way to make people read the Bible in hopes they would become Christian and abandon their own religious beliefs? Instead I chose to simply not return to the church and told them I would not participate in teaching English lessons.

After living out critical literacy with young children, I now understand Sahni's (2001) argument. Critical literacy is more about relationships on a micro level. I acknowledge that macro-level structures do influence and shape micro relationships. There are prevailing discourses circulating about appropriate ways children should talk to teachers and what it means to be respectful to adults. For example, in many Southern communities it is traditionally expected that children should have responded to Mrs. Adams, an adult, with a "Yes ma'am" when she told them to move off the bench. These macro-level discourses did influence the micro-level decisions and relationships in my classroom. Injustices we experience and witness seem to happen most often in relationships with others, many times people we interact with daily. Critical literacy then becomes a relational literacy with those people that we love and hold dearest to our hearts. This makes social action and speaking up harder to do at some levels. What do we do with what we witness?

CHAPTER 5

Whiteness

How Was Curriculum Shaped
by My Histories?

As I examine my interactions and curriculum decisions during teaching, I see how my beliefs and experiences shaped which questions from children I responded to and possibly the directions in which I took the curriculum. In this chapter I cast a critical eye on the decisions I made while teaching and how they were influenced by my history. I specifically reflect on interactions and choices where I might have failed to understand the experience of the Other, where I did not examine the norms or assumptions of Whiteness, or where I did not see the impact of Whiteness on marginalized groups. I contemplate: What did it mean for me to connect the playground experience with Rosa Parks's arrest? Did the critical topics I chose to bring up with the class reinforce privileges and assumptions of Whiteness?

CONNECTING THE PLAYGROUND BENCH INCIDENT
WITH ROSA PARKS

During the second week of the summer program, I shared with the children my observations of Mrs. Adams's demand that they get off the playground bench. After discussing possible alternative responses, I shifted the conversation in another direction. As I sat down at eye level with the students, I picked up a Rosa Parks biography (Schaefer, 2000).

CANDACE: I want to share with you a little bit; I'm not going to read this whole book to you. You might be familiar with this story. Her name is Rosa Parks. This is not a storybook; this is a true story. It is a biography. This really happened. I want you to listen and see if you really believe that this could have happened. To me it's quite amazing. We're going to look through the pictures mostly and do a picture walk instead of reading all the words. This is a picture of Rosa Parks. She was

born a long, long time ago in Alabama. . . . This is a timeline: so she
was born in 1913; that was almost 100 years ago. This was a picture
of her later in life.

HUNTER: Is she dead now?

CANDACE: Well, we're going to find out. This is the school that she went to.
Can you see carefully in the picture?

JENNIE: Ooooh, that does look really old.

CANDACE: It looks different.

JOEY: I don't see her. I don't see her.

A FEW STUDENTS: It looks old. Did she die?

CANDACE: We're going to find out. Let's see if the book tells us.

JENNIE: Yeah, she did.

By introducing Rosa Parks in relation to the playground incident, I was
trying to make a connection to an event about power that took place in
the South, where the children lived. On reflection I question this decision.
Parks's arrest happened well before any of the students were born. I thought
the students might have heard about Parks because the event happened geo-
graphically close, in a nearby city, and they lived in a city with a civil rights
museum. I hoped a connection would open up space for conversation and
contemplation about power differences. How else could my decision be interpreted? Is it offensive or inappropriate to put in the same conversation a
discussion about the African American struggle for civil rights with a teacher demanding children move off a playground bench? Now that I reflect on
this teaching decision, I see how my Whiteness shaped what I did. I did not
completely comprehend or put myself in the shoes of Parks (and other African Americans) to fully understand their struggle for basic human rights.

It seemed that the students' background knowledge about Parks was
limited. I shared my own opinion about the Parks' arrest up front: I stated, "To me it's quite amazing," referring to the point that laws were in
place to segregate people based on race. Even though I was very cautious
in most conversations to not share too many opinions for fear that they
might diminish the students' questioning and thinking, here I did vocalize
my opinion. Since I did not live during the 1950s and 1960s, it is hard to
imagine what life was like with blatant racism. It is hard to conceive city
life with signs designating where people could go to the bathroom, eat
their lunch, and sit on a bus. I am not naïve. Racism exists today, deliberate and covert. People's lives are still shaped by institutional systems of
oppression based on race.

From the beginning of our discussions, I contextualized the time period when Parks lived, which may have provided a space or rationale for
why the students felt distant from Parks. It immediately situated them after

her. I now think this played into the summer discourse as positioning racism and unfair acts as historical, not still happening today. As a child, I remember feeling disconnected from historical events, thinking that since I was not alive during the civil rights movement, I reasoned that therefore, I was not to blame. This remains a common perception among many today. It has taken years for me to unpack how White privilege is still circulating in society today. For example, African American mothers shared with me that they teach their sons to always get a bag for items they purchase in a department store because their sons are more likely to be questioned for shoplifting. I had never thought about this, as I intentionally reject the offer for bags, thinking it helps the environment. This demonstrates my privilege as a White person. It had not dawned on me that Other people experience shopping differently. Life experiences such as this one give credence to the idea that difficult conversations need to happen in schools. Discussions about events such as the bus boycott are necessary for younger generations to study; they are a part of who we all are.

When Hunter asked if Parks was dead, it began a series of persistent questions about her. This appeared to be an important question for the children, as Annie started off with the question in a one-on-one conversation with me the next day. This taught me how important it is for students to ask contextual, historical questions, much like adults do, in an attempt to situate themselves in relation to an event and/or person. It also demonstrates that children are curious to learn about other people's injustices. These students wanted to know more about Parks and her life. I did not answer their question about whether Parks was still alive—I did not want to give away what was to come in the book and was also unsure myself if she had died; I wanted to draw on another source to confirm before answering the students.

On reflection, I am not so sure that using children's literature was the best decision. By introducing Parks to the students, I shifted the conversation away from what happened on our playground to a historical figure the students did not relate to as much as I had hoped. Jennie commented on how old the picture of Parks's school was. The students could not seem to place themselves in the black-and-white photographs. Although my intention was to share with them another person in history who was asked to move out of their seat, as a place to investigate how Parks responded to issues of power, the conversation did not go where I had anticipated. Instead, the students distanced themselves from Parks and did not see a direct connection.

However, I question where else young children are to gain entry to a conversation about vertical power if teachers do not bring in historical examples. The idea behind my decision to connect Parks to our experience was to engender sensitivity to such matters at the place where students identify with the marginalized. Using children's books and historical examples was familiar to me as a teacher, so this is where I turned when making curriculum decisions. Looking back, I wonder how much this decision reinforced assumptions or a naive perspective. Did it perpetuate stereotypes or downplay the struggle of African Americans in the civil rights movement?

Unexpected Comments on Segregation: Feeling Uncomfortable with My Whiteness

During the next part of conversation, I introduced the word "segregation." Not sure the students recognized the word, I asked for suggestions on what it meant, hoping some might draw on background knowledge and images in the Parks biography. This was a shift from how I managed my prior language with the children: here I explicitly used the word *segregated*—a loaded word with a bleak history.

CANDACE: And then it says: in the United States they had segregation laws. What does it mean to be segregated?

HUNTER: That means when people tell you to move, you have to do it.

CANDACE: Well, that means people were in separate places. That means some people could not talk to other people (*used one hand to show division, separation*). Some people could only eat at some restaurants; other people had to eat at other restaurants (*using hand to show division*). I wonder why? (4-second pause)

HUNTER: Oh! This is like, like, the man, the man who got killed by the other guys (*seemed excited at first, then a sad voice tone toward the end of the sentence*).

CANDACE: For doing what?

HENRY: Martin Luther King.

HUNTER: Because, because, because, because he had a dream that um, um, um, that he said, he said Black people if um, he said that "I had a dream" and um "my dream is that people can eat at any restaurant they want to."

CANDACE: So this book reminds you of a man named Martin Luther King who had a dream that everybody could eat at the same restaurants?

Much to my surprise, Hunter articulated his thoughts on segregation drawing on the images in the text and prior knowledge. In the moment, I ignored his connection to King. His insight was accurate, as insisting people move was a part of segregation, but I had a set definition of segregation in mind and Hunter did not articulate it the way I was thinking. I realize now that my narrow definition and vision for the conversation got in the way of how Hunter was processing the concept of segregation. During the conversation, I attempted to embody, or to visually represent, what segregation is by using my hands to gesture. I did not bring race explicitly into the conversation about segregation, even though it was a fundamental component of Parks's arrest.

Hunter's interjection about King completely threw me off. Up until that point the students had never mentioned King. The sound in Hunter's voice when he said, "Oh!" and the hedging he used to talk indicated that he was simultaneously making a connection and had a difficult time putting his thinking into words. His voice began with the sound of happiness, perhaps because he was contributing to our conversation, but as he finished his voice trailed to a sad sound, possibly due to his realization of King's death. I wish I had asked him more about who "the other guys" are. Who did he mean when he referred to who killed King? But in the moment, I did not go in that direction. I was uncomfortable again with my Whiteness and the weight of King's death. I was unsure how to discuss this with children, many of whom identified as Caucasian.

Even, so, I reflected on how beautifully Hunter articulated King's dream, equating it to eating at any restaurant you want. This unexpected comment proved to be productive to our curriculum, as several times over the summer children brought King back into our conversations, making connections to our inquiry about segregation. In the moment, it indicated to me that Hunter had previous experiences either reading about King and segregation and/or hearing people talk about him. It signaled to me that children can talk about segregation, because I realized I was not the first to bring up this topic, at least with Hunter. Not sure where to go next, I brought the children back to the book: returning to the text was a safe haven for me.

Positioning the Self in Difficult Dialogues

CANDACE: So this book reminds you of a man named Martin Luther King, who had a dream that everybody could eat at the same restaurants? . . . And these people were not happy. Look at their faces, do you think they were happy because they were told they could not eat at the same place?

JOEY AND OTHERS: They were sad.

HENRY: They were um . . .

CANDACE: Do they look happy?

JOEY AND OTHERS: Sad or mad.

ANNIE: They're not mad.

CANDACE: You notice that they might be called African American people and they were not happy because they were told they could not go to the same places as people that had, who had (*pointing to self*) whiter skin than them. Do you think that was fair?

LOGAN: No.

CANDACE: You can see that they joined together in groups; they got together and talked about how unhappy that was. There was a law that told them that they were not allowed to sit in the front of the bus. Who got to sit in the front of the bus?

SEVERAL CHILDREN: The White people.

CANDACE: The White people did. Does that sound fair to you?

SEVERAL CHILDREN: No.

CANDACE: Look at the picture. Can you see how the White people are on the front? Where are the African American people?

SEVERAL CHILDREN: Back.

CANDACE: In the back. What do you think is going to happen when Rosa Parks gets on this bus?

The children were grappling with identifying how the people looked in the photographs. Up until that point, we had been looking at the pictures analytically and asking questions such as whether Parks was still alive or defining segregation. But here I shifted the conversation to embrace emotive language. I asked if the people in the photos were happy to be segregated. Some children responded in a more robotic way to my IRE (initiate, respond, evaluate) type of questions by saying "sad." In an IRE sequence, the teacher typically asks a question that she already knows the answer to, the student responds with what they think the teacher wants to hear, and the teacher responds with an evaluative comment toward the response (Cazden, 2001; Mehan, 1979). For example, I asked, "Do they look happy?" I knew the answer to this question, but I asked it anyway. The children responded "sad" and "mad." I responded with an evaluation confirming that the people were unhappy.

Toward the end of this conversation, we engaged in a series of IRE questions and answers. I felt like robots were responding to me. In contrast to other conversations we had, with a more dialogic essence, these machinelike responses frustrated me. I then used a typical reading comprehension question by asking the children to predict what might happen next in the story. Looking back, I wonder why I chose to use these robotic questions when they did not move our conversation forward. One thought is that I was comfortable as a teacher with IRE patterns, and I had begun to feel uncomfortable when the children began to explore the emotional aspects of Parks's arrest. I think now that responding to children in more dialogical, emotional ways that open spaces to question and wrestle with injustices would give children (and teachers) a space to share their beliefs and experiences.

I went on to ask about fairness. As an early childhood teacher, I had often heard children say, "That's not fair" when playing math games or at recess. My intention in asking about fairness was that the students would see the images in the book and what happened on our playground as unfair situations and open a space for conversation about inequities. I reasoned that fairness was a discourse that children understand, and therefore an entry point into deeper discussions.

In this interaction I also positioned myself with the "White" people who told African Americans where they could and could not go. I used gestures to point to myself when discussing segregation. This was a way to publicly identify with segregationists, as well as a way to show that even though I am White I do not agree with the actions of past generations in creating laws based on race. As educators, not only are words important to analyze but also gestures and body language; both are texts students read (Kuby, 2010). However, in positioning myself as an ally, I wonder where the children positioned themselves. Did they struggle to find themselves in this history, or did they even try? Finding and positioning the self in history, such as racial segregation, calls into question the essence of Whiteness for each individual.

FLASHBACK: A PERSONAL NARRATIVE
WITH WHITENESS AND SEGREGATION

My two elementary schools were citywide magnet schools, whereby students had to meet particular requirements to attend. The schools were separated in two buildings in different locations of the city (a K–2 building and a K, 3–5 building). Both buildings had kindergarten students from the neighborhood. The school building for the 1st- and 2nd-grade magnet classes was located in a Black neighborhood, even though most students at the school were from affluent White families. I do not remember driving through this neighborhood as a family; I only remember riding the bus to go to school.

The 3rd- through 5th-grade building was near the downtown area of our medium-size Southern city, in a neighborhood that was populated mostly by African American and low-income White families. The neighborhood was full of old houses and businesses. Most of my classmates were White and had reasonably comfortable lives in which their needs and wants were met. Since our school was not in our home neighborhoods, students were bused in from all over the city to attend.

As an upper-elementary-level student, one day I went to a part of the building I had never been before, curious as to what I would find. Walking down the staircase to a dark basement, I felt a sense of wonderment. I cannot remember the reason for walking down the staircase, but I vividly remember what I found. I discovered several classrooms full of children I did not recall seeing before: children who did not ride my bus, who did not attend school assemblies with me, who did not eat lunch with me, who were mostly Black. Are they always down here, I wondered? Who are they? By their size, I could tell that they were younger, not in an upper-elementary grade like me. It was confusing to me that their classrooms were in the basement—away from everybody else. Isolated.

LIVING OUT WHITENESS IN DIALOGUES

The morning after the class reading of the Parks biography, I was walking around the room preparing materials before school when a student, Annie, stopped me to ask some questions about Parks. She was having a hard time understanding why White people would create a law that forbade African Americans from sitting where they wanted to on a bus. We looked together at the biography and I pointed out some of the photographs that showed separate water fountains for Whites and Blacks. We discussed the photographs of African American people with angry faces. As the conversation continued, Annie kept asking why a law would be created that separated people.

Complexities of Race and Poverty

ANNIE: Um, how many years then, when Rosa Parks died?

CANDACE: When she died? We read from the Internet that she died three years ago in 2005. You were wondering why she didn't give up her seat, right?

ANNIE: Um, hum [yes].

CANDACE: Because this picture here shows her in it. What do you think?

ANNIE: (2-second pause)

CANDACE: Do you remember what we talked about the other day? (8) We talked about that—remember the people that were African American—they were not allowed to go to the same restaurants or drink out of the same water fountains. See here how it says "Colored"? That means people who were not White had to drink out of this water and other people drank out of the other fountains.

ANNIE: What does the White people drink out of?

CANDACE: They get a separate one by themselves. (4) What do you think about that?

ANNIE: Um. (2) Who was the poor one?

CANDACE: Well (*surprised sound in voice*), (2) I'm not sure who was the poor one. Do you have any ideas about that?

ANNIE: (4) Um, um (*nodded head indicating no*).

CANDACE: No? So what do you think: poor people should have one separate from other people?

ANNIE: (4) (*shakes her head no*)

CANDACE: Why's that?

ANNIE: 'Cause it's not really fair that, um, that the White people get to have their own drinks and they only get to drink out of this (*referencing the photographs in the book*).

CANDACE: What if the White people are poor?

ANNIE: (5) Um, I forgot (*slight giggle between both of us, as if there were an awkwardness*).

Annie approaching me before school with questions about Parks surprised me. This was only our second week together, and we had just begun to talk about Parks in relation to the incident on our playground. In the opening lines of our conversation, Annie taught me several things. One, I was struck by her beginning the discussion asking a historical, contextual question about how many years it had been since Parks died. Why would a child need or want to know this? This shows me she was probably wrestling with a sense of time and maybe trying to figure out where she belonged, if at all, in the Parks story. I remember asking similar questions as a child when I heard stories about segregation and the struggle for civil rights. Conceivably Annie was unsure of her role or responsibility as a White person in this story about racial segregation, similarly to how I questioned as a child. To Annie, it was important to situate her curiosities about Parks within a time frame.

She also taught me that young children ask similar questions to those that older children and adults ask, such as questions about time, death, and context, to help us understand our relationships to events. Her pointed questions in this excerpt demonstrate the sophisticated ways a child can talk about important historical events and people. Throughout this interaction there were long pauses, indicative of the delicacy of our conversation, Annie's thoughtful articulation of questions and comments, and our uneasiness with discussing racial segregation as Whites. Still, Annie was insistent to ask questions and to continue the conversation instead of shying away from troubling concepts.

When Annie asked, "What does the White people drink out of?," she may have been trying to find herself in the story of segregation again, situating her own identity as a White person in the book images. She continued by asking about poverty, which took me by surprise. We had not discussed the issue of poverty at all; it was the first time that race and poverty were connected in conversations. This interaction with Annie taught me that children are able to hypothesize about larger issues in society. By looking at the images in the book and possibly her previous life experiences, she was trying to process how race and poverty could be related. This may have simply been a reflection of her culture and own privileged Whiteness, in which "poor" and "Black" are often referred to synonymously, even if it is a misconception.

In these opening lines, Annie also showed how the intellectual work of understanding racism is deeply tied to emotion. Even though she did not verbally use words or phrases such as "sad," "bad," "happy," or "I am feeling," Annie did indicate her feelings of how hard it is to talk about segregation and how it did not make sense to her as she gazed at the images in the book, through long pauses and indicators such as hedging. She articulated her feelings that it was unfair to separate people at water fountains. This experience with Annie supports the idea that the so-called line between analytical, rational reasoning and emotion, especially in critical literacy, is blurred (Boler, 1999). Annie draws on both to process these injustices.

There were a lot of pauses and what appeared to be sincere responses, such as "I forgot." This demonstrated that Annie was really interested in pondering the questions I was asking her. However, as a teacher I leaned on what I was comfortable with, the children's picture book. As I read her expressions, a quiet demeanor and perplexed face, I was confused. I remember thinking: How much do I say? How far do I push the topic of segregation? Do I share my opinions, or do I allow her to grapple with this issue on her own? When does this line of questioning in critical literacy become mine and no longer hers? I was internally wrestling with the pedagogical idea of letting children construct their own knowledge. I thought if I shut her down by answering her questions with my opinions, then a curricular space would not be opened for further conversations.

After revisiting this interaction, I noticed how much I was talking. Why? In the moment, the pauses and moments of silence made me uncomfortable. These pauses indicate that my ideologies on segregation and poverty were creeping into my mind. I was struggling with how to model empathy and to have conversations, as a White woman, on deep social issues like racial segregation.

"You Would Give Up Your Seat?": Placing Annie on the Bus

CANDACE: So what happened then? See how they were angry because they felt they weren't getting treated the same as White people. Then what happened? Remember [what] we talked about? Who gets to sit in the front of the bus?

ANNIE: (5-second pause) The White people.

CANDACE: The White people and it says the Black people had to sit in the back.

ANNIE: Why?

CANDACE: Somebody made a law like that. That said that. Why do you think men would make that law?

ANNIE: (4) What's men?

CANDACE: Men or women. Why do you think man or woman would make that law?

ANNIE: Hmm. (10) I don't really know.

CANDACE: Does it sound like something that would be fair? If you got on a bus and saw that all the African American people had to sit in the back, how would you feel about that?

ANNIE: Um. (4) If I was the White people?

CANDACE: Um, hum [yes].

ANNIE: Um. (3) I would let them sit in my spot.

CANDACE: You think so? What, what if *you* were an African American person? (*imaginative voice tone*)

ANNIE: Humm.

CANDACE: How would you feel?

ANNIE: (4) Hum, (1) bad (*hard to understand—maybe "sad"*).

CANDACE: You might feel sad to sit in the back. Do you think that's how they felt back here? (*in book*)

ANNIE: (nods yes)

CANDACE: Possibly? Have you ever ridden on a bus before?

ANNIE: (nods yes)

CANDACE: Is it really hot and bumpy on the back of the bus?

ANNIE: (nods yes)

CANDACE: Yeah, it's not as comfortable as the front where the air could be. Yeah? So you would give up your seat if you were a White, if you are White, which you are, right? You'd give up your seat if there were some African American people who needed a seat?

ANNIE: (nods yes)

CANDACE: You think so? (4)

As this conversation continued, Annie's responses taught me more about how children can contemplate a topic such as segregation, especially when they are wrestling with their own Whiteness. Annie seemed a little unsure, and as her teacher, I wanted to connect the photographs in the book of segregated water fountains to what we discussed previously about bus segregation. I found myself offering support by asking her to remember what we talked about the day before: "Who gets to sit in the front of the bus?" I responded with what might be considered developmentally appropriate; I was trying to make connections to class discussions.

Annie taught me in this snippet of conversation how persistent and curious she was about why people are segregated. She asks, "Why?" Annie lives in a time period that does not segregate people by law on buses, so the photographs in the book are hard for her to process. They do not fit with her own experiences. Annie, trying to connect Parks's experiences to her own, continues to go after the question of "why." This was similar to my questions over the years as to why students were separated in my school basement. Why would adults knowingly separate the neighborhood kindergarten children, who happened to be African American, from the predominantly Caucasian children?

I remember questioning if I should tell Annie my opinion or let her continue researching to discover possible answers. In this instance, I decided to tell her, "Somebody made a law like that." Annie was still stunned and perplexed by this law; after a long 10-second pause, she said, "I don't really know" in response to my questioning. Instead of offering me a teacher-friendly response, an answer that would please me, she put herself out there and openly struggled.

As the conversation continued, I once again leaned upon my understandings of early childhood pedagogy, asking Annie to make connections to her own life. I inquired if she had ever ridden on a bus before. My intention was to talk about what it feels like to ride in the front of the bus versus the back. Why might White people have preferred the front? One reason could be because it is more comfortable to sit at the front of the bus, but another reason could be because of status. I was hoping Annie would think about why the front of a bus was a more desirable place to ride.

I found myself toying between the real and the imagined by asking if she would give up her seat as a White person. In the moment I clarified her identity as a White person after the previous interaction, where she questioned her identity on the bus while we verbally role-played possibilities. I stumbled over my word choice, hesitating to label someone's identity as a White person. What if she did not identify with the White people on the bus? We each have multiple, fluid identities, and it was not my place to categorize and choose Annie's identities for her, although in the moment I did. As a teacher, I realized the sophistication Annie had in thinking simultaneously of the here-and-now and the imagined possible perspectives as a way to help her (us) better understand segregation.

Admitting When You Don't Understand

Later in the conversation, Annie circled back to Parks, and this time we explored possible reasons for Parks not giving up her seat.

CANDACE: All right, any other thoughts about Rosa Parks?
ANNIE: Um, how come she had to not give up her seat?
CANDACE: How come she *did not* have to?
ANNIE: Um, hum [yes].
CANDACE: What do you mean? (*said quickly*)

ANNIE: (4) Like how come she didn't give it up for the White man?

CANDACE: Why do you think? What do you think was going on in her head when the White man came and asked her to get up? What do you think she was thinking?

ANNIE: She was thinking not to.

CANDACE: Why? What would be her reason? (*higher tone in voice*)

ANNIE: Because she wanted to keep her spot because that was her spot and I think that she knew that (2) you shouldn't share your spots because whoever gets there, you get to ride on the bus on that seat.

CANDACE: So she decided to say no, huh?

ANNIE: (2)

CANDACE: And when she decided to say no they put her in jail. Because they thought because she was African American that she did not deserve to have a seat on the bus.

ANNIE: Why not? (*naïve curiosity in her tone*)

CANDACE: (2) I'm not sure why not. I think that the White men felt like they had more *power*. (2) What do you think? Do you that people who have White skin should have more *power* than people who have a different color skin? (4) Hummm . . . that's tough.

ANNIE: That'll hurt their feelings.

CANDACE: It would hurt their feelings, wouldn't it?

ANNIE: Um, hum (yes)

CANDACE: That's something I still don't understand either, Annie, why they would make a rule that said that. (4) Hum. Any other thoughts?

The bus segregation law did not make sense to Annie; blatant segregation did not fit into her experiences and perspectives on fairness. My response to Annie was to have her think about what Parks might have been thinking the day she was arrested. I believed that Annie, even as young as she was, could take on various perspectives. She responded with the idea of "first come, first served." Perhaps to Annie, it would have been fair for Parks to share her seat literally, moving over to share the seat with another person. But because she was forced to get up, in Annie's opinion it was not fair.

Toward the end of the conversation, we revisited the idea of consequences of actions and rights. Annie continued to push me as well in the conversation by asking, "Why not?" After a pause, I answered that I was not sure. In this instance, I remember thinking: Do I respond in an open-ended way for Annie to have space to explore her own inquiry, or do I finally tell her my beliefs? I chose to share my beliefs here, hoping this would somehow give her more to think about and possibly push our conversation forward. Reading the emotions through Annie's tone and hedging, I was able to see how difficult this conversation was for her. I resonated with her and expressed how tough this was for me, too. Even if people rationalized the law of bus segregation, to Annie it did not feel right. Annie was concerned with how oppressed people on the bus felt. She stated, "That'll hurt their feelings." She empathized with a group of people, not the same race as her, even though her own racial group oppressed (and oppresses) them.

As we shared our feelings and beliefs, I opened up to her that I, too, did not understand the situation. As much as I wanted to have conversations with children about injustices, or at least observe how they talk about injustices, I did not realize how difficult it would be for me, and perhaps the students. In moments such as these, I found myself consciously filtering every word and response, debating in my mind what would be appropriate to share (although there is not consensus on this by adults) and what I wanted to leave unsaid for Annie to wrestle with on her own.

Seeking Additional Perspectives

As we neared the end of the conversation, Annie decided that she was not done talking about this and wanted to talk more with the class, which caught me off-guard.

CANDACE: Well I'm going to stick this (*the book*) back up there (*on the shelf*). And do you want to talk about it anymore?
ANNIE: What?
CANDACE: Do you want to talk about it anymore today or are you okay?
ANNIE: Um, I want to talk a little more today (*quick response, no hesitation*).
CANDACE: Right now? Or with everybody else?
ANNIE: Um, with everybody else.
CANDACE: What would you like to ask? What are you still wanting to know from other people? (4) Hum?
ANNIE: How come Rosa Parks, um, had to give up her seat?
CANDACE: Why does she have to give up her seat? Because . . . you want to see if anybody else can help us figure that out?
ANNIE: (nods yes)
CANDACE: Okay, we could do that. Will you help me start that discussion with everybody else?
ANNIE: (nods yes)
CANDACE: Okay.

In the last part of our conversation Annie taught me that even if she had not discovered an answer to her question she still wanted to pursue it later, among her peers. This was a question she believed was worthy of a longer discussion, because she did not feel that she had a firm understanding of the topic. I asked Annie if she wanted to talk about it any more that day. I wanted Annie to know that I was okay with her discussing it at school; I wanted to give her more space to converse if needed. Did she tell me she wanted to talk about it with everyone in response to my prompt or because she genuinely wanted to hear her peers' ideas? Even though I was the teacher, typically seen as a knowledge-giver, Annie was not satisfied with what she gained from our one-on-one interaction. We ended our conversation; I put the picture book back on the ledge of the whiteboard and waited for other students to arrive. I was energized from our conversation but a little apprehensive and excited about what was to come in the class discussion.

On reflection, this conversation served as a powerful lesson of the sophisticated ways children can wrestle with social injustices. Annie appeared to be seeking a relational connection to Parks through her empathetic questions and comments. It was not evident to me in previous years of teaching how children can talk about injustices, because I had not listened. Surely children were talking about injustices, but I did not take the time to embrace their curiosities that might have appeared inappropriate for children. Children conceivably did not feel comfortable enough to bring up issues like segregation, or I did not model this type of emotionally invested intellectual conversation with them. Even though I valued conflict resolution and had students talk through their problems, I did not explicitly open spaces for dialogue about larger school, community, or worldwide social injustices. Reflecting on my own childhood in the South, I realize I did not have spaces like these with my teachers, either. Annie did not shy away from dialoguing about racial segregation, even while struggling with her own Whiteness; she sought to have space to process and dialogue about this history.

MOMENTS OF CONSCIOUSNESS-RAISING

Isolated. Is this how the kindergarten students felt in the basement of my elementary school? Is this how Rosa Parks felt on the bus? Is this how my students felt as they walked, with their snacks in hand, away from the playground bench? Is this how I felt as a teacher of children wrestling with the uncertainties and tensions of a critical literacy curriculum specifically with topics such as racial segregation? Is this how Annie felt talking with me before school?

As a child, walking down to the basement of my school, I felt like I had done something wrong, like I was not supposed to be there. What I found, then, was such a surprise. Why did I not know these children? As a young girl, I had used pens and pink highlighters to make notations in my yearbooks of my friends across grade levels—people I knew from riding the bus, from church, my friends' siblings, and from other extracurricular activities. There are photographs of students with hearts around their pictures or comments in the margins. But the pages of the kindergarten students are blank, without marks of endearment. The entire 1st- through 5th-grade pages had smiling faces of mostly White students, girls with big bows in their hair, braces on their teeth, and the latest fad of clothing. But the section of the yearbook for kindergarteners, mostly African American neighborhood children, was without markings.

Now, years later, I still have mixed feelings and thoughts. I am angered and frustrated that somehow it was rationalized to segregate children within a school of mostly relatively wealthy White children even in the 1980s. Why? In conversation with my mother, she tried to remember why. She thought it was because the school district wanted to keep the kindergarten children in their neighborhood school. But what happened to these children in 1st grade? How was it explained that they could not go to their neighborhood school for the rest of their elementary years? Were they bused into a variety of other elementary schools in the district in an effort to integrate the schools? Where were the voices of their parents? Were they okay with their children being bused out of their own neighborhood so that wealthier, mostly White children could attend a magnet school? I acknowledge that my writing depicts my perspective of the situation, however, these questions leave me frustrated and uncomfortable.

I wonder if I was the only student in my school who realized how different the kindergarten classes were. Did other students walk down the staircase to the basement? Did anyone else question this but not have a space in class to discuss it? While the discovery in the basement puzzled me at the time, I do not remember asking someone else about this as a child. It was not until years later, as a graduate student, that I began to reflect on this moment and the ways it influenced me, even if I was not conscious of it.

On a deeper emotional level, while teaching I saw myself in the students from the summer program. Was the one-on-one conversation with Annie or the class discussion *really* about Rosa Parks for me? Probably not, as the law had already been changed. It was more about acknowledging and allowing a curricular space for children to verbally wrestle with this injustice. It was about coming to know one's own Whiteness—the privilege, position, and power that are inherently there. It was more about wanting children of relative privilege to see or experience other viewpoints. However, is this the space where critical literacy becomes dogmatic, or is it about exposing children to a range of perspectives?

In a class conversation, the children responded, "I don't know" when I asked them why a law would be created that separates people. Should I really have been surprised that they did not know why that law was created? Do adults really understand segregation, either? Sure, we can understand it based on studying power and hegemony or listening to the lived experiences of Others. However, really understanding racism and segregation is not easy—for a White person. As I unlearn my Whiteness, I see how it is hard for me to understand racial segregation, as I have experienced privilege because of my race. Questioning if segregation can be understood is a statement reflecting a White privileged mindset.

As a child I questioned why people were segregated in my elementary school basement, much like my students questioned the bus segregation in the book. How different might my beliefs be today if I had an experience or space to problem-solve about the kindergarten children in my school the way these children began to think about bus segregation? How might having a space to dialogue and verbally role-play about what I saw in the basement have helped me as a child to process the situation? To begin to understand my Whiteness?

Even though I felt uncomfortable about my discovery, it seemed "normal" to separate children because nobody—that is, the adults I trusted—talked about it. I probably felt that if nobody else was talking about it, then it must be all right. I pondered the same question that Annie and the students did. Why would a group of people make a rule that separates another group of people, in this case kindergarten children? Even though I was not consciously thinking about this childhood moment while I was teaching during the summer, I believe that on a deeper level it affected how in-tune I was to Annie's queries and why I supported her in bringing the issue to her peers for discussion.

I believe my childhood experiences impacted how I responded to Annie's inquiry on segregation. I was more in sync with her persistent questions about Parks, possibly over another child's curiosities, because they reflected my own inquiries. I could relate; I found myself in Annie. Therefore, I made spaces in our curriculum for her comments and questions because they so closely aligned with my experiences. The process of autoethnography, specifically on examining Whiteness, allowed me to become aware of the people, places, and experiences as a child and young adult that shaped who I am. These moments of consciousness-raising shape how I approach teaching. It is crucial for teachers to take time, however emotionally difficult it might be, to dig into their past to bring to the surface personal ideologies and biases that shape their teaching (and lives as a whole). We must interrogate our own upbringing to know where we come from, especially in relation to the privilege (or oppression) of Whiteness. Whether we identify as White or not, we are all affected by how Whiteness positions us.

CHAPTER 6

What Is a Negotiated Critical Literacy Curriculum?

In this chapter, I explore the notion of a *negotiated* critical literacy curriculum. As an early childhood educator I was familiar with the idea of a *generative* curriculum, in which the curriculum is decided on together with children based on watching their play, listening to their talk, and having conversations about their interests (Fisher, 1998; Helm & Katz, 2011). As I began to read about critical literacy, I resonated with Vasquez's (2004) notion of co-creating inquires with children where critical literacies are "negotiated *as* the curriculum or *into* the existing curriculum," not as an add-on or isolated event (emphasis in original, p. 32). Although I believe that curriculum should be co-created with children, it is worthwhile to closely examine what that looks like in practice, when tangled in a web of power relationships and ideologies.

Vasquez (2004) describes how she listened to children's conversations in the schoolyard before the school day began for issues and topics to explore. Each morning the students set an agenda of how they would be learners during the day (i.e., who would work on what tasks as part of larger inquiry projects). While Vasquez was a part of setting the day's agenda, students also had a voice in determining what their learning would look like—the curriculum was negotiated.

Comber et al. (2006) share another example of negotiating critical literacy curriculum. They demonstrate urban renewal from the inside out when students participated in a redevelopment process, negotiating and redesigning the land area between the elementary school and a preschool. Students researched with architects and community members and proposed ideas of how the space could be used. The curriculum was negotiated daily as children worked to have their voices heard about how to use school space.

Readings such as these give insights into how critical literacy inquiries are negotiated. I sought to create a classroom environment where I listened to topics and issues that children talked about and ways to co-plan our learning time. However, in dialogues about racial segregation and power dynamics on our playground, I was not comfortable with how much to say about my beliefs. I wondered if I was being dogmatic or simply trying to help the children see multiple viewpoints.

In this chapter, I share experiences from my childhood and young adult years about power relations and belief systems that influenced my learning. I also discuss excerpts from my teaching journal, to indicate the constant struggle in negotiating a critical literacy curriculum with students and how teaching decisions are connected to ideologies.

Reflecting on my own teaching during the summer program, I wonder how negotiated the critical literacy curriculum really was, even though it was my goal to try to co-create inquiries with the children. While it was not my intention to teach critical literacy from a dogmatic stance with the children, I now wonder how co-negotiated the curriculum around Rosa Parks and the playground bench really was. Even with intentions to negotiate, how did curricular decisions really get played out? How did my ideologies and experiences shape what I allowed or did not allow in the official curriculum?

FLASHBACKS: PERSONAL NARRATIVES OF EXPERIENCING DOGMATIC TEACHING

As a teenager, I remember sitting in the basement of our church's youth center on Wednesday nights. I had strong affection for my teachers and always enjoyed going to Bible study classes. However, I also questioned in my heart and mind what I was hearing. The Bible seemed to contradict itself a lot, particularly when read literally. Parts of it seemed oppressive, which made me uncomfortable, especially since many such references were toward women. I did not feel that I was allowed to question any of this out loud, however, because the Bible was presented as "the Truth." There was a circulating message that it was the "inerrant word of God" and therefore unquestionable. As a child I internalized the message that I was supposed to take what was written in church literature and the Bible at face value and suppress my questions. I learned that the church curriculum was not negotiable.

As written in Chapter 2, I traveled with my church youth group on mission trips during the summers. While these trips served as a time away from our families to have fun with friends, they were also a vehicle for wealthier White people to "save the souls" of those less fortunate than ourselves. What message does this really send? I felt like a colonizer (a term I did not understand fully until my graduate work) as an middle-class White girl sweeping in to "save these poor souls." I encountered the same feeling living in Japan, when a church I visited a few times wanted me to help with

English lessons by using the Bible. By choosing to participate I would not have been valuing Japanese religious belief systems, instead implying that my religious traditions were correct, and imposing an unfair use of power (the power of knowing English).

These vignettes are experiences I encountered where curriculum and readings were presented as a singular truth. They are also examples of times when someone with more power, usually an adult, decided the curriculum or "truth" for a child. From my perspective, there were not opportunities for me, other children at the vacation Bible schools, or people in Japan to question the texts used or how they were interpreted.

TENSIONS OF PLANNING CURRICULUM BASED ON STUDENT INTERESTS

After talking with the children about the playground bench incident and reading the Parks biography, I was not sure which direction the inquiry would follow. I did not intend to spend the summer talking about Rosa Parks and racial segregation, but I also did not expect the line of questions about her that the children asked.

> Today we revisited the problem about the playground. On the chart I had written out from [yesterday's] videotape [of our class conversation] the ways they could handle that problem: what they could do, what they could say. Some students brought up the question of where rules or laws come from. We were talking about who makes the rules and laws for the playground. Some said parents and some said the principal—so they are not really sure where these rules are coming from. So that might be an angle or way to take [the curriculum] next. . . . They were interested in seeing if Rosa Parks was still alive today, and if not, how she died. So, that might be a possibility of something that I can talk about with them. Um, so um, I'm not sure where to go next. I'm not sure if we should spin off this [racial segregation] [and focus on] Rosa Parks, or if we should look at the rules on the playground and where those come from. I'll have to think about that for a little while and where to take it next. (Teaching Reflection Notes, Wednesday, June 11)

This journal entry illustrates how I toyed back and forth with how to negotiate a critical literacy inquiry with the students. Should I have helped them understand where laws come from (like the playground rules), or should we have explored racial segregation once they were asking questions about Parks? As this was a summer program, 6 weeks can be viewed as a long time, but on the other hand it was a short amount of time to develop an in-depth inquiry and foster conversations from a critical literacy stance. As the next journal entry captures, we did not have time the following day to explore either of these directions because university practicum students had lessons to do with the children.

> Today we just ran out of time; we didn't have time for me to share the article I printed about Rosa Parks, and we had so many adult [university] students in the room it was hard to get to anything besides math games. . . . I think that the playground thing has kind of sizzled and died, so I'm thinking that I should start on Monday by sending home cameras, having them share about their homes, where they go, and things they do [to see if this sparks a direction for us to inquire about, any critical literacy topics from their communities] . . . . Um, and see where that takes us next. (Teaching Reflection Notes, Thursday, June 12)

Once again, this audio self-reflection shows that it was not clear to me what to do next. I felt the playground incident was a nonissue to the children, but did not want to abandon the questions children asked about Parks. My original intention before the program began was to send home cameras as a way to get to know families and possible issues in their communities that we could research from a critical literacy stance. The preceding journal entry captures my decision to go in that direction and let the playground and racial segregation topics fizzle. But then Annie came into the classroom the next morning with very specific questions about Parks and racial segregation, which changed the curriculum path (see Chapter 5 for the dialogue with Annie).

> A really interesting thing happened this morning. Ellie and Annie, the twins, came into the room first and we had a few minutes by ourselves. Because Annie had been the one who asked me if Rosa Parks had died or not, I showed her how I had printed out some information about her and the date of her death . . . She's having a hard time understanding why White people would create a law that forbid African Americans from sitting where they wanted to on a bus. She wanted to know if we could bring [this question] up to the whole class to see if we could get any clarification. But when we brought it up we really didn't get an answer as to why. So I'm thinking maybe on Monday

to read a picture book about forbidding people to have library cards and maybe explore the history of some other things like the right to vote. Henry thinks that [racism] was a really, really long time ago but maybe that's something else I can bring up. Helping him see that it was probably during the time his parents were alive or at least his grandparents. So they can get a sense that it wasn't a very, very long time ago that it is still very real. Um, so that's where we are. (Teaching Reflection Notes, Friday, June 13)

The conversation with Annie was pivotal on many levels. I remember thinking carefully about the words I chose to respond to Annie's questions. On the one hand, I wanted to help her understand power relations and the roots of segregation; on the other hand, I did not want to be dogmatic. I also wanted her to have questions to explore and research on her own about segregation, instead of me supplying answers. I was shocked that she wanted to bring her questions back to the class for further discussion, but decided that I could not deny her this opportunity to facilitate a conversation about her inquiries. After the class conversation around Annie's questions, I decided to introduce other picture books that discussed racial segregation beyond bus laws, to offer other perspectives of how African Americans were treated during the years leading up to the civil rights movement. My hope was that discussions would surface, for example, about power relations and injustices around rules made for African Americans in libraries, restaurants, and bathrooms.

Today I read the story about Richard Wright's library card and tried to see if that would help to process maybe some reasons why White people would create a law that did not allow Black people to do certain things, but the children just didn't [come up with reasons]. They had a lot of fruitful discussion, but we still can't find an answer [about why a law would be created to separate people]. So maybe I'll start tomorrow by posing to them, um, how reading books gives us knowledge, and maybe how that can give people power to think differently. . . . Then I might maybe think about reading another book . . . that talks about racism and see what happens from that; um, see where it goes from there. (Teaching Reflection Notes, Monday, June 16)

This audio self-reflection captures my hesitancy. On the one hand, I wanted to give children space to wrestle with their questions about racial segregation. On the other hand, I was not sure how much information from the Internet and children's books I should share. I found several other picture books that had themes related to race, some with young children as characters, that I thought they might be able to relate to better.

Today I read *Sister Anne's Hands* [Lorbiecki, 2000]. Before I read it, I talked a little bit about the book from yesterday, *Richard Wright and the Library Card* [Miller & Christie, 1999]: a little bit about what books give us—they give us knowledge and information—and how that makes us smarter. We talked a little bit about how we think that maybe White people were afraid of African Americans becoming smarter than they were. Then I read *Sister Anne's Hands*, and one phrase stuck out: "Roses are red, violets are blue, don't let Sister Anne get any black on you." [Some students] really thought that people's skin could wipe off on them. So we had a few friends in our class who are African American rub their hands on somebody else and notice that their skin does not change colors when they touch someone else. And we talked about how that note in the book was a very mean thing to do. We are still trying to figure out why the parents of the children in Sister Anne's class did not want them in there. We are talking a little bit more about fear. I'm thinking of somehow maybe talking about that again tomorrow. Maybe reading one more book and seeing kind of where they go with that next. Also introducing the learning wall [the audit trail to document our inquiry]. I photocopied the fronts of the books we've been reading and wrote comments from our conversations about what we're making sense about [related to the critical literacy inquiries]. So, maybe sharing the learning wall with them and seeing if they have any more ideas of stuff we can add to the wall. (Teaching Reflection Notes, Tuesday, June 17)

Today we read the book *The Other Side* [Woodson, 2001], and were talking about if they had ever noticed a time in their lives when something was not fair because they said it wasn't fair that the girls could not play together that were on the different sides of the fence. At the very end [of the conversation], Sam made a comment that he knows in Mexico people who are poor aren't treated fairly either. [I'm thinking he might have visited Mexico before and is making this generalization.] That might be a way to start a conversation to think about other people who are not treated fairly. Not because of their race but because of other reasons such as their income levels. Henry thinks these books really happened a long time ago and the students do not think that racism is still happening today. (Teaching Reflection Notes, Wednesday, June 18)

It continued to trouble me that the students felt racism was no longer present. Here, my ideologies about systematic racism butted up against teaching decisions. I questioned how much to let thoughts like this slide, or how much information to give to help expand their perspectives and recognize their own privilege in society—many of whom do not experience racist acts. Part of me wanted to protect their perception of innocence, while the other part of me knew that by the diversity of the class there were probably children or families who had experienced racism. Should I silently move on to another topic and perpetuate a narrow-mindedness that subscribes to being color-blind (a stance that parent questionnaires seemed to reinforce at home)?

The very act of having an African American child rub his or her skin on a Caucasian child is problematic. I hoped it would dispel the myth that skin color wipes off. However, even in the moment of asking a child to wipe his or her skin on another child, I wanted to take my words back. Who was I to pinpoint a child's identity as "Black" (or another other race) in front of the class?

Charting Out Our Thinking: Big Ideas on Racial Segregation

To help us process and revisit the ideas of the books we read, I decided to create a large chart. The first column of the chart described what happened in the book; the second column captured whether we thought the situations were fair or not and why; the third column described why we thought the situation happened; the fourth column suggested what could have been done differently; and the last column listed other questions we still had. We spent several days revisiting these books and having conversations about whether we thought the actions were fair toward groups of people and why. The hard part was the "why." The children struggled to articulate why parents would separate their children playing on different sides of a fence, why parents would not want their children in Sister Anne's classroom, and why Richard Wright was not allowed to have a library card.

> I'm trying to pull them back to Henry's idea about racism happening a long time ago and thinking about things that have happened to them more recently. So, how things are still unfair and unjust in the world right now—I'm wondering if they could be in small groups and maybe draw or chart somehow their writings and drawings, something that's unfair that's happening to them that they've seen. Maybe not to themselves but to other people and maybe use those as some discussion points of things that happen currently. Maybe I should bring in a newspaper even and look at some things in the newspaper, um, as a way to help them think about current things that are unjust. Also, maybe using Sam's comment about poor people in Mexico or talk to Henry about his thought about voting for Barack Obama and see where that goes. (Teaching Reflection Notes, Thursday, June 19)

The discourse throughout my reflections depicts the constant negotiation through modal phrases such as "maybe," "I'm wondering," and "we'll have to see." Modal phrases, the use of hedging words, indicate an uncertainty and how uncomfortable I was in discussing social issues such as racism. I was playing around with possibilities for the curriculum. Yet at the same time, I struggled with how to follow the students' questions and introduce them to new topics, ideas, and events in history. My own Whiteness and position in society kept creeping into my mind—is it appropriate for me, a White woman, to discuss racial segregation with children? Of course it is, I thought; if children do not have spaces to discuss aspects of history, such as the civil rights movement, does history have a chance of repeating itself?

Voices on the Bus: Exploring Multiple Viewpoints

After multiple days of conversation, I wanted to help the children see beyond one perspective. Many of them articulated that they would never treat someone the way the books described. However, I wanted them to know that the situations described were complex and that not all people during the civil rights movement felt the same way about the laws. I decided to create a learning engagement that would provide space for them to take on various perspectives on the bus the day Rosa Parks was arrested. I read aloud the book *Voices in the Park* (Browne, 2001). In this picture book, two families of gorillas travel to the park: a mother and her son and a father and his daughter. The book is divided into four sections, or voices, of each character. The sections use different images and fonts to tell the story of visiting the park from each character's viewpoint. We spent a couple of days reading the book and discussing what we noticed. I explained to the students that we were going to use the text structure of the book to write a text about the incident on the bus the day Parks was arrested. I divided the children into four groups: Rosa Parks, the White bus driver, the other African Americans, and the other White people. Each group met with my teaching assistant or me to brainstorm words for their assigned voice. We used images in a variety of picture books as a springboard for the children to begin to think about what each group of people might have felt and experienced. Using graphic-organizer webs, we captured the conversation of each group and used the webs to type the text (see Figure 6.1).

The aide and I both agreed that this [process] was very hard for them. . . . A lot of children looked through the picture books and that was helpful for them to see illustrations of African Americans and how their faces looked. They kept talking about how Rosa Parks was not lifting

FIGURE 6.1. Graphic Organizer Web for Voices on the Bus

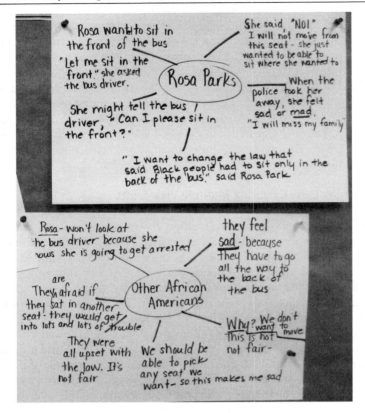

her head or looking the bus driver in the eye. [Students] were talking about how they [other African Americans] were afraid of getting arrested. That maybe the other White people did like African Americans but they were also afraid of getting arrested. That is why they did not speak up or do anything. Um, so it's a really hard issue to grapple with especially in a small group and knowing *how* to lead the discussion and what to say next. . . . It is hard for them, I think, to imagine what it's like or to put themselves in someone else's shoes. Some of them were able to grasp on to that but for some of them [I wasn't] quite sure if they were catching on to the whole idea of taking someone else's perspective. (Teaching Reflection Notes, Thursday, June 26)

Even though I was unsure at first how this activity would go, I was astonished at how the students were able to pull apart various perspectives in complex ways. For example, in the section from Parks's voice students not only stated that Parks felt the law was unfair but also articulated that she might have felt sad because she knew her choice to boycott could result in an arrest, which meant she would miss her family while in jail. The students realized that Parks might have contemplated the consequences of her actions. Parks was hopeful that the unfair law might change but was aware that there could be negative repercussions such as separation from her loved ones. This demonstrated the complex ways young children can pull apart and hypothesize perspectives.

Another example comes from the section written from the voice of the bus driver. Students hypothesized that even if the bus driver felt that African Americans should have equal rights, he might have been too afraid to stand up for them because he felt pressure from the law and might have been afraid to lose his job. The group that wrote the section from the voice of the other White people on the bus thought there might have been at least two perspectives: some who were jealous that their seats were taken by African Americans and some who felt the law was unfair but were scared to say anything because they could get arrested for speaking out. The group from the perspective of the other African Americans focused on their fear of getting arrested and how they observed Parks's movements, such as her not looking the bus driver in the eyes (as indicated in a picture book). Within each of these groups the students were able to play around with possible viewpoints.

> Today we finished painting the illustrations for the Rosa Parks book. . . . We'll be able to put it together and read it on Monday for the first time. Then I'm thinking of reading *Henry's Freedom Box* (Levine, 2007) or the American dream [book] that Henry brought up as a way to talk about a more historical perspective and what things happened in the past, but also then talking about today: what is the hope, what do we hope for, when we talk about issues of racism. So hopefully that will be where we go next week. Then the last week I'll have to see maybe if we should explore other issues of fairness that are happening to us right now. Um, it just feels like I need more and more time, because they keep asking questions and we keep moving forward with it. (Teaching Reflection Notes, Friday, June 27)

I struggled to know how far back in history to go in how African Americans were treated, especially when students had some background knowledge on people (e.g., Martin Luther King Jr.) and events (e.g., slavery, immigration from other countries), which they talked about to the class. These comments raised more questions from their peers and gave spaces to explore areas I had not thought we would discuss.

Through all of this, I struggled with my own identities as a White female who did not live during pre-Civil War slavery and the civil rights movement. Did I have enough knowledge to facilitate conversations with young children? How was my Whiteness limiting or reinscribing notions of oppression? Even though my privileges might not allow me to know how someone else experiences the world, I decided that is not cause to avoid conversations and potential action with children I teach. Being uncomfortable and experiencing tensions is not a reason to remain silent.

INQUIRIES THAT DID NOT BECOME A PART OF THE CURRICULUM

In attempting to negotiate a critical literacy inquiry with the children, it goes without saying that I was not able to allow official curriculum space for all the children's questions. As a teacher, I made decisions on which inquiries to explore further as a class. These decisions were not easy, as so many of the children had questions that stemmed from either discussions around racial segregation and/or the playground incident. Time is limiting. I was not sure what to pursue further and what to let fizzle.

> Today we revisited *Henry's Freedom Box* [Levine, 2007]. We took a picture walk through it, discussing what had happened. We used a graphic organizer to chart what the problem was, if we thought it was fair, and what could be done differently. We talked a little bit about greed and how the White people bought the slaves to help them to be more profitable in their factories and their farms. They talked a little bit about how the law should be changed but none of them are really sure about how it came about. . . . I also showed them a map of the world and we talked about how the African Americans came over on boats and how the Europeans, the White people, came over from Europe and England. Henry knew a little bit about England and how they wanted to leave because they didn't like the rules there. We then looked at America and talked about how there were other people already here first, the American Indians or Native Americans. It was interesting because they wanted to know why White people would come over here if the Native Americans already lived here. We talked about the conflict and how the Native Americans didn't like people coming to the land that they were already on so that might be a place to go next with them also. (Teaching Reflection Notes, Wednesday, July 2)

I have not been able to go to the library and get any books about England invading America. I'm not sure if I'll be able to, because the librarian wants all the books back by Wednesday. The kids did not seem as interested in [this question, as the boy who originally asked it is not here this week], so it might be something to move on from. (Teaching Reflection Notes, Monday, July 7)

Within a negotiated curriculum, when a teacher is listening to children's curiosities, there are tensions with what questions get brought back into the official curriculum for further explorations and which ones do not get revisited. Teaching is not neutral; it is ideological. One child had questions about European settlers invading Native Americans' territory. Another child mentioned that African Americans came over on boats, but I did not clarify or challenge him to consider that they were kidnapped. Instead of following up on these remarks, we continued to investigate racial segregation and the incident on our playground. As the previous reflections mention, there were several reasons for this decision on my part. One, the boy who commented on Native Americans was not there for several days after he asked questions and other children did not bring this topic back up. Second, as the program was ending soon, the librarian had asked for books to be checked back into the library, and we had limited resources (as we did not have access to the Internet). Third, I wanted to circle back to the playground event and connect our weeks of discussing power issues related to racial segregation to the power issues on the playground. In any case, I made a decision to not follow up on his line of inquiry.

MOMENTS OF CONSCIOUSNESS-RAISING

Much like what I experienced as a child at church with questions about the Bible and what adults told me, my students also questioned the materials they were presented about Parks, segregation, and their own experience on the playground. I hope the difference is that as a teacher I attempted to give them curricular space to question situations they perceived to be unjust. As a child, I did not feel that I had permission to question the teachings at church or even at school. How do educators create spaces where children know that questioning is acceptable or even necessary for learning? Inviting children to question, as I believed was important, also created tensions and uncertainty. Knowing where to go next with the critical literacy inquiry was difficult, and my decisions were tied to my ideologies and identities. Negotiating curriculum happens within the culture and context of communities of learners, all of whom have identities, experiences, and beliefs.

What happens when children experience vertical power relations and social injustices and we do not give them space to deconstruct and reconstruct these relationships? For me, I suppressed my uneasiness with an exclusive faith for many years. Not until adulthood did I find spaces and relationships that allowed me to openly question religious doctrine. As a child, it was normal to go on summer trips and be expected to talk to people about Jesus. Even though this made me uncomfortable, I felt that questioning it was not allowed. In fact as a young adult, when I expressed to peers that I did not want to travel as a missionary, I felt judged. I felt like I was supposed to have dreams to travel and save people's souls. These were experiences of vertical power relations between adults (sometimes even peers) and myself. I did not want this to be the case in my classroom. I intentionally wanted children to ask questions about injustices, power, and how the world works. As educators, do we honestly invite children to question what they read, see, hear, and experience? Do we present singular truths to students simply by our actions? How do we really include children in making decisions about curriculum? What *is* critical literacy teaching?

Teaching in the summer program helped me examine what a negotiated literacy curriculum is. Through struggling with how much to say about my opinions and sticking with my agenda, I contemplated what does not get discussed—the decisions teachers make *in the process* of teaching and interacting with children.

> I think one thing I've realized this summer is it's hard when you get on a topic like this: how do you know how far to go, how far to take it, and when it's been exhausted? . . . I think it's a very fine line of listening to children and trying to figure out where they are and what other direction you can push them to think about something they might not have been exposed to yet. How do you know when it's too much for them? (Teaching Reflection Notes, Thursday, July 10)

It is productive for teacher education programs to encourage teachers to first unpack their ideologies that influence teaching decisions, and second to embrace the messiness of not sticking to a lesson plan or agenda. Educators must also acknowledge how policies and mandates, which teachers often feel restricted by, influence how negotiated a curriculum is. How can educators advocate for negotiated curriculum in a climate of restrictions? To truly negotiate teaching, we have to be ready to muddle through children's questions and be prepared to co-create curriculum with them (even if it diverges from our plan). We have to find ways to advocate for student-led inquiries, even in a climate of scripted and mandated programs. At the very least, we have to acknowledge how our own identities and histories influence curriculum.

CHAPTER 7

"We, Them, White, Black"
What Language Should Educators Use?

In this chapter, I explore the language I used around issues of segregation, racism, and power between teachers and students, and the broader issue of language in a critical literacy curriculum. The language I chose to use during the summer program connected to the labels I heard growing up. As a teacher, I struggled with words such as "we" and "they" in reference to events in books we read about segregation. Terms such as White, Black, and Brown were used to describe groups of people. Did this reinforce the misunderstanding of race as a skin color rather than as something socially constructed? Relationships are experienced through interactions and language. Throughout teaching, I was inconsistent in my talk with the children in labeling groups of people. I have since thought about the implications of my language and why I simplified racism through language. Did my language position some groups as better than others? Were the words I used the easiest way to discuss difficult topics with children? Language is not neutral; as educators it is crucial to become aware of how language positions and possibly hurts people.

Brian Street (1984) writes of two types of literacy: autonomous and ideological. The autonomous perspective views literacy as context-independent and neutral, and values universals. Sometimes this perspective gets lived out in the practices of policymakers, textbook publishers, and testing companies—that literacy is neutral, and that there is one right way to read and respond to texts. Students' unique cultures, communities, and experiences are not taken into account. The ideological perspective views literacy as situational and context-dependent, social and cultural, and embraces the particulars of various literacy practices. This perspective acknowledges that people use literacy in multiple ways in their communities. Educators who foster spaces for ideological literacy practices find ways to include the varied literacy practices and cultures of their students. Critical discourse analysts extended the conversation on ideological literacy to include language. James Gee (1996, 2005) and Norman Fairclough (1989, 1992) write about the ways language is not neutral—power, position, and privilege are all lived out in both oral and

written discourses. Perspectives of these educators influenced how I ana-
lyzed my own discourse with students and the language I experienced (and
participated in) as a child.

FLASHBACK:
A PERSONAL NARRATIVE OF OTHERING THROUGH LANGUAGE

I have many memories of sitting on the swing or in rocking chairs on the
porch of the home I grew up in as a child. It was a joyous place of eating ice
cream, watching lightning bugs, saying hi to neighbors who were on evening
walks, and telling stories. As a child I remember hearing my family recap
events from the day—people they came into contact with at work or school,
events in the news, or something they read. Not until college did I begin to
think about our discourse when telling stories. Many times my family pref-
aced stories with "African American" (or "Black") and "Mexican" when
describing people. As a child, I saw this as a descriptor much like someone
would use words such as tall/short, young/old, woman/man, and so forth.
But are these neutral terms?

Using terms to label the race of someone has broader implications. It
demonstrates that White is normal, as we did not use White to describe
anyone in the stories; it was assumed. It also assumes that by saying Black or
Mexican, specific connotations about a person's character, lifestyle, or experiences are understood. By doing so, for example, the language homogenizes
all Black people as having the same experiences and/or lifestyles, which is
not accurate. Language is not neutral.

As I studied about language being socially constructed and how words
are ideological in nature (Fairclough, 1989; Gee, 1996; Street, 1984), I began
to see labels a little differently. I wondered how stories would be received if
I told them without using such descriptors. Would it be any different if I did
not preface a narrative with "Mexican"? I started to see how descriptors are
ideological and not only apply to race but also sexual orientation, religious
affiliations, and other ways of labeling our complex and multiple identities,
which socially are valued in different ways.

LANGUAGE TO DOWNPLAY INJUSTICES

During conversations with the children, the language I used made Rosa
Parks's arrest seem like a nice event where she was kindly told to get up
out of her seat, omitting discussion of the law behind the actions and the
violence of the civil rights movements around this event.

CANDACE: I was thinking that people were asking you to get up and lose your seat [on the bench]. It reminded me of another lady who was on a bus one time and who was asked to get up out of her seat and move. Have you ever heard of someone who had to get out of their seat on a bus and move?

SEVERAL CHILDREN: No.

HENRY: Yes, I have before. Well, my mom said, um, I have to sit up out of the seat and then I can, I can sit on my mom's lap.

CANDACE: Okay, so maybe if there are lots of people who want to sit down, you, because you are small enough, could sit in your mom's lap, [allowing] someone else to have a seat?

I found myself using "nicer" language to talk about what happened to Parks, simplifying the horrific treatment of African Americans. Was she really *asked* to get up out of the seat? There was a law behind the actions of the bus driver and police officers; legally, it was not really a choice. This is one example of managing my words with the children and the difficulty in choosing language to talk about such injustices. My choice of language downplayed the injustices African American people experienced (and continue to experience) daily.

MANAGING THE CHILDREN'S LANGUAGE

An example of managing the children's language happened in a discussion about the teachers telling the students not to sit on the bench.

CANDACE: Yesterday we had a discussion about an issue on the playground and I wrote it up here [on chart paper]. It says "problem." The problem I noticed on the playground last week is that we wanted to sit in the shade to eat snack but sometimes people asked us to get up off the bench that was under the tree. We talked about how some of you were not very happy to have to move when you had unpacked your snack and you were eating in the shade. Some people gave us other ideas of places that we could sit in the shade. Henry told us under the slide might work. And he also said maybe you could also sit on the ground in front or behind the bench on the rocks there because there is still shade. And some people said to sit by the door: the sidewalks [are shaded there].

JENNIE: And the little benches.

CANDACE: You're right, there were a few benches that were red benches. They are a little shorter but are also in the shade. Okay? So those are some other options if we're really hot and want shade. And then some of us said, these are some things you can say (*pointing to chart*) to people if they tell you to get off and you don't want to get off. You can tell them, Jennie said, that it is already full. There's no space and you were already there first. Joey told us we could tell friends to "back off."

FEW STUDENTS: (*laughter*)

CANDACE: Now, people might not be happy to hear that but you could say that in a nicer way. Joey? How could you say that in a nicer way?

JOEY: Can you get off?

CANDACE: Ah, so that sounds so much better (*talking while writing*). Can you please get off (*laughter from children*)? Okay, so if you want to sit there, Joey, that would be a way to say it. Henry said we might just say, "Scoot over," there might be enough space if people kind of squish together.

By telling Joey to think of a nicer way to respond to the bench incident, I managed his language. I also filtered my language and chose a nicer way of describing what happened on the playground. The teachers did not really ask the students to get off the bench; they told or demanded. In the moment, this shows how uncomfortable I was talking about this inequity between a teacher and students, especially with other adults present in my classroom.

As I read Joey's suggestion to tell people to back off if they ask to sit down there was a low rumble of laughter in the room as students realized this is not an appropriate way to handle a situation. The students, especially Joey, taught me how easy it is to apprentice or mentor students in appropriate, socialized ways of responding to conflict through the language used. I asked Joey, "How could you say that in a nicer way?" My hope as a teacher was if the students could find a way to articulate their thoughts and feelings in an "appropriate" (or nicer) way, maybe the adults on the playground would consider their response. I knew that it was a touchy subject to try to get children to voice their reactions to a request made by an adult. I wanted to help him find a nicer way to respond because I wanted to protect him from getting in trouble or getting his feelings hurt by the teacher. My response was to control or manage his language so that he would learn how to respond in what might be perceived as an acceptable way.

I have mixed feelings about how I responded. I slowly said the word "please" as I wrote it on the chart, emphasizing the word as a nice gesture. Part of me realized that helping Joey find a polite way to respond to the teacher might help him have a positive response from Mrs. Adams if she asked him to move in the future. But at the same time I was conflicted, not wanting to squash his language and voice in problem-solving. However, I noticed how I inserted the word "please," as this was not Joey's original language; I added this to his response. This is an example of how I demonstrated what I perceived as an appropriate way to communicate in conflict.

"EASY ANSWERS" TO TOUGH QUESTIONS

While many of our conversations about the bench or Parks seemed to be honest wrestling with difficult topics, sometimes I felt that the students gave me a teacher-friendly, easy, or expected response (see Chapter 5 for a discussion on IRE interactions), highlighted in the following conversation about racial bus segregation.

ELLIE: It doesn't matter the color of their skin.
CANDACE: It doesn't matter? Oh, well, it seemed like it mattered (*looking at whole group with my hands out in a questioning position*) to the people who made the law. Why do you think it mattered to them?
JOEY: They were sorry. They were so sorry.
CANDACE: They were sorry to make that law?
JOEY: Yeah, so they won't do it again.

This short exchange is an example of how conversations shift between what appeared to be deep wrestlings to robotic, parroted performances. Ellie previously stated her belief that skin color does not matter, which is the first time someone voiced an explicit comment that skin color (i.e., race) should not matter in bus seating. I challenged her because I wanted to bring the students back to the segregation law that Annie was questioning.

Joey's comment at the time seemed cute and what someone might expect from a child. One might anticipate an early childhood teacher to praise him and agree that they were sorry in order to steer clear of this topic. However, I continued to ask questions. Joey's comment that "they were so sorry" reminded me of a previous conversation when Hunter shared that at his school they let Brown and White people sit in the front of the bus. I asked the class if they thought it was fair for both Brown and White people to sit in the front, then asked:

CANDACE: How do you think it [being able to sit up front] made the Brown people feel?
HUNTER, DERRICK, AND A FEW OTHER VOICES: Good.
CANDACE: How about the White people?
HUNTER, DERRICK, AND A FEW OTHER VOICES: Good.

CANDACE: So they were sitting together. . . . It was kind of like a group
    hug.
GIRL'S VOICE: And then if someone wanted to sit in the back they could sit
    in the back.
CANDACE: Then anybody could make that choice, right?
DERRICK: Yeah, if somebody wanted to sit in the back they can. And the
    White people say, "You want to sit in the back."
DERRICK AND ANOTHER VOICE: Or they could stand up.
CANDACE: Or some people could stand up.
DERRICK: And some people say "yes" I want to sit in the back. (2-second
    pause)
CANDACE: Well, we still haven't answered Annie's question. Annie's ques-
    tion is: Why would White people make a rule or a law that makes
    people that are a different-color skin sit somewhere different? And we
    haven't figured an answer out for that. Is that something we can think
    about? Some of you said we might find an answer on the Internet.

Some responses, like "so sorry" and "good," appeared robotically performed; the students were giving me what they thought I might want to
hear. Joey knew that when you do something wrong you are supposed to
apologize. Especially for children in the early childhood years, adults often
condition students to apologize when there is conflict, even if they do not
understand what they have done "wrong" and many times when they really are not sorry (Wohlwend, 2007). By stating this, it appeared that Joey
was positioning himself as a "good" student, telling me what he thought
I wanted to hear. In some ways norms in early childhood education support this notion that the teacher's role is to manage emotion and language.
Teachers are supposed to help children learn how to interact socially and
work through conflict. Within this line of thinking, the teacher should keep
things calm and balanced. Therefore, my role would be like an orchestral
conductor, directing a symphony of emotions and words. Reflecting on this
short interaction has taught me to critically examine my own practices of
working with children during conflicts and difficult conversations.

"WE, THEM, BLACK, WHITE, BROWN": WHO AM I REFERRING TO?

One of the most troubling aspects of language was trying to figure out what
words to use to describe someone's race. At times I used the term African
American, while at other times I used Black or Brown. However, White appeared to be the only term I used to describe Caucasians. In conversations I
lumped people together using terms such as "we" and "they." Who is that?

Who does it include and exclude? In the example below, we were problem-solving rules that would be fair to all people on buses.

CANDACE: But why did they do it [create a law for racial bus segregation] in the first place?
HENRY: But guess what . . . If the bus driver let the Black people sit in the front and the White people sit in the middle of the bus and the Brown people sit um, like um, at the back of the bus that would be fair too.
CANDACE: Why would that be fair?
HENRY: Because they would each have their own seat.
CANDACE: How about if we put. . . .
HUNTER: . . . But you. . . .
KATIE: (raises hand)
CANDACE: . . .Yeah, Katie.
KATIE: Um, well, at my school when we go on a field trip our class always goes in the middle.
CANDACE: So your whole class sits in one place together, it doesn't matter what color your skin is, right?
KATIE: (nods head yes)

The students continued to contemplate the concept of fairness. Henry complicated our discussion more by verbalizing a rule for not just two groups of people, but three: Black, White, and Brown. Adding the term Brown to our conversations is troubling. What does Brown even mean? Who might belong in this classification system that Henry articulated?

As indicated, Henry believed as long as people have their own seat it was fair, no matter if it was in the front or back of a bus. I hesitated to express my disagreement with Henry, afraid it might shut down our conversation, so I nodded my head slowly in acknowledgment. I know the language of "Black," "Brown," and "White" homogenizes groups of people. I wrestled with how to make space available to talk about injustices such as segregation without putting people in categories and stereotyping.

Trying to get the students to unpack the power relations not only on the bus but also on the playground, I found myself using pronouns to assume how students identified themselves in these scenarios.

CANDACE: When you are on the playground or anytime that someone asks you to get up and move. Do you think that people asked you to get up and move on the playground because of the color of your skin this week?
LOTS OF CHILDREN: No.
CANDACE: Why do you think people asked you. . . .

LOTS OF CHILDREN: (*overlapping, inaudible speech*)

HUNTER: Because they want to sit in the shade!

CANDACE: Because they wanted to sit in the shade?

ANNIE: Because they um, wanted to sit down and they didn't want to sit in the sun because they wanted the other people's spot.

CANDACE: So, if we want everyone to have a chance in the shade. . .

LOGAN: They're being mean (*quietly, almost inaudible*)

CANDACE: We thought of some different things we could do (*points to chart on the board*), right? There are other places to sit. Do you think it was just to be mean? Logan thinks they were just trying to be mean.

SEVERAL CHILDREN: (*overlapping, inaudible speech*)

CANDACE: What do you think?

JENNIE: Yeah, because . . . the bench is already full . . . nobody can sit there.

CANDACE: This is true. Well, all right, I have some other books up here that you can look at later if you'd like to read more about Rosa Parks.

Here I attempted to compare both events with regard to issues of power. Even though we did not go into depth here about power, we did talk about race and power more as the summer progressed. Upon reflection, I have trouble with this conversation. I explicitly asked the children if they thought they had to move off the bench because of the color of their skin. I made the statement because I wanted them to see, in my opinion, that they were asked to get off the bench because of their age—they are children and adults claimed to have more power, privilege, and position to sit on the bench. However, when making this statement I did not consciously take into account the African American children sitting in the room during this lengthy discussion about Parks. Did they identify with her based on their race? Did they connect race to the playground incident? They might have really felt that race was the reason a teacher asked them to move. Assuming children think a particular idea based on their race is not fair or accurate. How do I choose my words such as "we" or "they" when I do not know how children identify themselves?

Hunter somewhat surprised me. He gave such an obvious reason to my question about why people asked them to move off the bench: "Because they want to sit in the shade!" This also demonstrated to me that he was not thinking beyond the surface reason, to deeper beliefs on adult/child relationships. As a teacher I wondered if I should not push this discussion further. Maybe it was a dead subject because they did not feel oppressed on the playground.

Logan, almost inaudibly, said, "They're being mean." In the moment, I did not ask him whom he was referring to. It appears he was referring to the people who asked them to move off the playground bench. Was he identifying them with the mean people in Parks's story? Over the next several weeks Logan did not vocalize much about his thoughts and feelings toward the playground incident. However, Logan opened up to me during a one-on-one conversation the last day of the program about how he felt about Mrs. Adams and the events that happened on the playground (Kuby, 2013c).

When I brought Logan's comment back to the class, Jennie responded with "Yeah, because . . . the bench is already full." I agreed with Jennie and Logan, articulating my opinion that basically the way the other teachers handled the playground incident was mean. This positioned me from the beginning of the summer as an ally to their cause. They knew up front that I disagreed with them being forced to move off the bench.

Dialoging with children about social issues such as racial segregation is tricky. Language is not neutral, and therefore the words teachers choose to use matter. Beyond references of racial labels, pronouns include some people and exclude others, and situate people within categories. We position students and ourselves with the language we use.

NEW VOCABULARY

I also struggled with vocabulary that students were not familiar with and how to discuss new terms such as *slavery*. I noticed the students wanting to know more about the history behind racial bus segregation, so I read aloud the book *Henry's Freedom Box* (Levine, 2007) as a way to introduce them to the history of slavery and racial segregation. These notes taken from my teaching journal indicate tensions.

> Today I read *Henry's Freedom Box* and I also showed them a very simple timeline so they could see that *Henry's Freedom Box* happened a long time ago and they could see where Rosa Parks fell in place. . . . I think that some of them were kind of getting it but I think it was definitely a difficult topic, lots of new words like master and slave. They didn't quite understand, but some of them knew what they meant and it was helpful. (Teaching Reflection Notes, Tuesday, July 1)

As children asked questions about Parks and related issues of racial segregation, I wanted to give them curricular space to explore history. However, as they asked about how and why segregation laws were implemented, I felt the students needed a broader historical understanding of relationships between Caucasians and African Americans. By reading books, I introduced new concepts and words to students such as *slave* and *master*. Once again, I found myself carefully filtering my language.

When dialoguing with children about issues such as racial segregation, how do we speak directly about difficult topics such as race and slavery without oversimplifying complex issues? Do we perpetuate stereotypes and beliefs of race being equal to skin color instead of socially constructed? Finding vocabulary that children understand yet that does not maintain oppression and misunderstandings is not easy.

VERBAL ROLE-PLAY: HEDGING AROUND WITH POSSIBILITIES

I found myself hedging or using modal words (e.g., *might, maybe, perhaps, possibly*) when discussing difficult topics with children. This was a way to provide space for students to think without me telling them my opinions or because I really was unsure how to respond to some of their questions, comments, and worldviews. In a previous vignette, Joey told the class that we could tell friends to back off, referring to one way of responding to the demands about the playground bench. Not wanting to silence his ideas, I grappled with what to say next and chose to use language that nudged him in the direction I wanted him to go. I stated, "people might not be happy to hear that but could you say that in a nicer way, Joey? How could you say that in a nicer way?" Using words like *might* and *could*, I thought, would come across as less judgmental, but ultimately I was managing the words and actions of Joey.

Another example of the students and me using modal words when discussing difficult topics happened in the one-on-one conversation I had with Annie before school (see Chapter 5). In this interaction, I fell back on the belief that it is important to start with the familiar when working with children, so I set up a role-play situation where she was on the bus with Parks. My intention was to ask Annie how she would feel on the bus. To my surprise, Annie had already role-played a different identity than hers as a Caucasian girl and had opened herself to the possibility of position-taking. She asked, "If I was the White people?" This short question is so powerful. It demonstrates that at a young age Annie was able to move beyond an egocentric mind and take on multiple perspectives even before I asked her! I asked her to consider if she were an African American person, how it would feel to be an African American in that situation. The hedging in my voice and drawn-out words, "what if you," indicate that as a teacher I really pondered what to do next. We used words such as "might" and "if" along with long pauses, perhaps because we were both aware of the difficult nature of the conversation. Her response took a little more time, but she was able to articulate how bad it would feel to be forced to sit in the back of the bus. In the moment and upon reflection, this interaction is still very powerful. In early childhood education, one perspective is that it is difficult for children to take on multiple viewpoints because they are egocentric. However, here Annie decided that drawing upon verbal role-play and positioning herself in a range of perspectives was helpful in her processing. She made this decision without me initiating it! Perhaps my use of modal words gave permission to role-play possibilities and not search for one right answer.

My use of hedging as a way to process teaching decisions was also evident in my audio notes. I used the space each afternoon driving home to process my thoughts while talking into an audio recorder. This space allowed me to play around with different pedagogical decisions as I reflected on the day. My own language demonstrated the need to use modal words as a way to process something difficult, teaching from a critical literacy stance. I was role-playing possible teaching directions through language.

MOMENTS OF CONSCIOUSNESS-RAISING

We construct language socially, which implies that meanings are not fixed but are situated within time and space in particular communities. My own Whiteness, histories, and experiences, such as the conversations on the front porch with my family, shaped the language I used with the students. Closely examining the discourses of the classroom alongside readings on language and race helped me understand how words position people. Language in classrooms (and society), according to Gee (2005) are "little d" discourses. However, discourses become ways of being tied to belief systems and power, which Gee terms "big D" Discourses (Gee, 2005). Language is ideological (Street, 1984). At first I did not think twice about using words like "we" or "them." However, as the summer went on, I began to catch myself while talking to children, trying to figure out what language was best. I think back to the language I heard as a child growing up; "Black" and "White"— race was mainly presented as dichotomous. What happens when children, especially of privilege, hear identity labels such as these presented as one or the other? Does it perpetuate an "us-and-them" mentality with "us" being better? Does the discourse of "White" and "Black" shape the Discourses of a family and community? I believe so.

So do we not talk to young children about race? I do not think so. These conversations, even if difficult, need to happen in our society from a young age when ideas about race are forming. But the question remains, how do we discuss social topics without simplifying the issues too much or not presenting a realistic, multiple, and complex picture of history? Having candid conversations with children about how groups of people have been (and continue) to be treated is important, especially if we aspire to live in a more just society. Helping children see multiple viewpoints (i.e., that not all African American people have the same views or experiences) also helps to break the us/them perspective. Children need spaces in schools to discuss difficult topics like race, sexual identity, expected gender roles, and poverty (to name a few). The language we use in these conversations is crucial in how ideas and understandings are constructed.

Now I find myself stopping to think about descriptors like "White" and "African American" when I tell a story about someone. I still struggle, depending on the context and relationship of the person I am talking with, to decide whether to use "White" or "Caucasian" (or "Black" or "African American") for example. I understand that race is inextricably tied to one's identities. Is a racial label even needed to describe someone when telling a story? If so, is the label always needed or only in some circumstances? How does the label influence the story or how someone perceives the person I am talking about?

CHAPTER 8

We Didn't Approach Mrs. Adams
Can Social Action Be Embodied Over Time and Space?

In this chapter, I explore what social action is in critical literacy inquiry, especially with young children. Most critical literacy scholarship focuses on larger social action projects such as creating petitions or surveys, acting out a drama to share various viewpoints on an issue, or planning an event in a community with people who hold positions of power, which are all worthy endeavors. However, as I began to teach from a critical literacy perspective, I questioned what social action means, especially in early childhood. Is it more about social transformations between people? Are there more subtle, even personal forms of social action that as teachers we might not visibly see the result of in our classrooms?

As I revisit the memory of walking down the stairs to my elementary school basement, I question why this moment is so sedimented into my memory and why I did not approach an adult about my discovery if it was so pivotal. Is there any social action if I did not speak out and question what I witnessed? First, I have processed why I did not speak out. I felt powerless as a child to question adults who made the decision to place African American children in the basement and not allow them to participate in schoolwide assemblies, field day, or dismissal procedures. The adults I trusted in the school knew that all of these children were in the basement classrooms. Did they view this as problematic? In my elementary school, curricular space was not about questioning or dialoguing about things students witnessed in our community. School was about filling out worksheets, reading leveled texts, and obeying the teacher. School was not a space where children could expect time to wrestle with injustices they experienced or to question things they saw in the news or the town. I internalized these expectations.

Even if this was the case for how school operated, I am not comfortable in thinking that social action did not happen as a result of my discovery in the basement. This moment did change me. What effect does this moment in my history have on me, even as an adult? Is there any social action from these experiences 25 years later? How am I still changing because of this event, decades later?

Even though the students and I were together only for 6 weeks, were there opportunities for them to take action? Could social action happen in literacy engagements, while painting or participating in role-play? Just as I noticed that social action related to events in my childhood did not come to fruition until years later as an adult, were there embodied moments of social action (perhaps not evident until months or years later) in the critical literacy inquiry from teaching in the summer program? Yes. Social action is embodied in relationships over time and space.

SOCIAL ACTION THROUGH MULTIMODAL LITERACIES

Literacy is multiple and situated in the practices of particular communities (Street, 1984). I understand literacy to be more than alphabetic communication through written print or oral language. For example, literacy also includes art, embodied emotions, song, movement, gestures, media, and performance. Therefore, I created opportunities while teaching that encouraged children to use multiple literacies to communicate their ideas and learning. Multimodal literacies, as described by Pahl and Rowsell (2012), are a way of teaching and learning that embraces all "modes within texts of all kinds" (p. xix). For example, children can use multiple modes to share their learning of research on a topic: clay sculptures, painting a mural, designing a website, writing a poem, performing a script, creating a podcast, and so forth. In this chapter I argue that social action is multimodal and lived out in relationships and literacy practices over time.

Social Action Through Composing, Writing, and Illustrating

During the fourth week of the program, I noticed that my students had a difficult time thinking of varied perspectives related to the complicated issue of civil rights. I hoped to create a learning engagement that would provide space for critical conversations and an opportunity for students to explore and represent their understanding of bus segregation. As described in Chapter 6, I read aloud the book *Voices in the Park* (Browne, 2001), with the intent of the class authoring a parallel text about the day Parks was arrested. In groups we used images in picture books and verbal role-play (Kuby, 2010) as ways to hypothesize what these people might have felt. I typed the written text based on the group discussions, and each child illustrated one page using a black permanent marker and watercolors.

The students began to see that not all people felt the same about this complex event in history. I also shared a book (Adler, 1995) about Parks that described how about a decade before the famous bus incident, Parks encountered the same bus driver. She was asked to get off his bus and to use the back door instead of the front door even though she had already paid her fare. I shared with students how she made the decision years later, as part of a larger collective movement, to purposely get on the bus knowing she might be arrested.

Next are several examples from *Voices on the Bus* that demonstrate children taking social action among their peers and teacher to articulate their understandings of an injustice. These images demonstrate children's understanding of power relationships and segregation; these are a form of social action. Students made declarations as multimodal designers in how they drew the scenes using colors, size, positionality, and lines to show emphasis. These images are a powerful visual literacy in which students demonstrate social action through composing and illustrating a book (Albers, 1999; Kuby, 2012, 2013a, 2013b).

Hunter authored a page (Figure 8.1) for the portion of the book from the perspective of the White bus driver. The text for the page he illustrated said, "I looked around and saw that other Black people had sad faces because Rosa was getting arrested." Hunter drew four people as brown (African Americans) with what appeared to be streams of tears falling to the ground. The fifth person, much smaller in size, was painted yellow with a blue hat, which is assumed to be the bus driver. Hunter also used speech bubbles to capture the voices of the African American people such as "sad" and "waaay" (sound of crying).

My eyes were drawn to the large, numerous tears falling and the distinct frowns on the faces of the African Americans. The combination of the frowns pointing down and the tears streaming to the ground took my eyes to the bottom of the image. This evoked a heavy sadness and stirred up anger because of the oppression African Americans experienced. The use of speech bubbles with words such as "sad" and "waaay" combined with the tears evoked empathy. A viewer can smell the saltiness and moisture from the tears, can feel the tears rolling down the faces, and hear shouts of frustration. These emotive aspects from Hunter's illustration demonstrate embodied social action—he used this painting as a way to communicate to his peers and teacher the empathy and disagreement he had with bus segregation.

Carson was in the group that authored the section from the perspective of the other African Americans. The page he illustrated said, "We noticed that Rosa wouldn't look at the bus driver because she knew she'd get arrested for not giving up her seat" (Figure 8.2). In his illustration, he painted three people. On the left side a woman, presumed to be Parks, stands

FIGURE 8.1. Hunter's Illustration

FIGURE 8.2. Carson's Illustration

looking straight at the viewer. Her body is colored brown with blue arms. Carson used yellow to highlight the area around the pupil of her eye. The middle person is assumed to be the policeman, with a large hat and yellow arms and legs. His arms are pointing to Parks. The third person, on the far right, is sitting in a seat, presumably the bus driver. The skin is painted yellow with purple clothing.

Carson demonstrated a sense of agency and knowledge of politics in his illustration. Most visible was Parks resisting the bus driver and policeman. She was not looking them in the eyes and seems to have distanced herself from them. This demonstrated Carson's understanding of the peaceful, nonviolent means of resistance prevalent during the struggle for civil rights. He was politically aware of Parks's choice to boycott the bus law and appeared to understand the hierarchical power among these three people. Carson's social action was to clearly articulate his understandings of Parks's choice to not look the driver in the eyes (as indicated in several photographs of Parks in the picture books we read)—as a way of protesting and making a statement in a nonviolent way.

While the children did not share this book with a community at large (i.e., other classrooms and parents), they did share their beliefs about bus segregation in front of peers (myself and other adults in our room). Many students had not verbally expressed their ideas about segregation in class discussions; however, illustrations gave them an avenue to take a stand on bus segregation and voice the ways they felt the law was oppressive and not just. Even though I placed them in groups for the four perspectives on the bus, children expressed their beliefs in unique ways by decisions on whom to include in their paintings and the use of size, colors, positions, and facial expressions.

As Sahni (2001) argues, critical literacy in the younger years is more about relationships than about large macro projects. I sensed this in the paintings of *Voices on the Bus*. Students risked how their peers and teachers might perceive them when they made decisions while painting. They knew the paintings would be public within their classroom—that we would read the book as a class. This, too, is a form of social action; even though subtle, it should be acknowledged and valued as social action nonetheless. Speaking out with those closest to you is sometimes harder than going to a large protest where you can blend into a crowd. These children risked relationships to articulate their beliefs about injustices, possibly because I created this learning engagement for all to participate in or because they felt reassured that this type of dialogue was accepted in our room. It is my hope that over time and space their experiences taking on multiple viewpoints related to the bus boycott will shape how they respond to other injustices.

Another example of using visual literacy as a way to socially act comes from the last day of the summer program. Logan and I had a conversation about a painting he was working on about the playground bench experience (Figure 8.3). I asked the children to make a painting with two panels: on the left side an unfair situation they experienced, and on the right side how they might respond differently in the future, focusing on peaceful ways to respond. Logan chose to paint about his experience on the playground bench, which was somewhat surprising since he was not vocal in class conversations about his experience. Even though Logan did not have a conversation with Mrs. Adams, the teacher who told him to move off the bench, his painting allowed him to publicly share with peers his feelings about being told to move. This experience demonstrates embodied social action through painting.

Through our conversation together and by looking at the details in his drawing, I was able to better understand how he felt about the situation. Prior to this conversation, Logan had not explicitly expressed his feelings about the teacher and bench scenario. A multimodal response provided a way for Logan to socially respond to the incident and to imagine new ways of being in relationships. Children speak loudly about their feelings through the details, the placement and size of objects, and the colors chosen in their drawings (Albers, 1999; Kuby, 2013a, 2013b; Van Leeuwen & Jewitt, 2001). Logan used his painting as a way to role-play possible solutions and to perhaps bring about social change in the future.

Social Action Through Role-Play

Another example of embodied social action comes through verbal role-play as I read *Sister Anne's Hands* (Lorbiecki, 2000) out loud (see Chapter 6 for more discussion about this interaction). This story portrays the difficulty of an African American nun teaching at a Caucasian Catholic school. As I read, the students had lots of questions about nuns, Catholicism, and angels. In the book, a student writes a rhyme on a paper airplane and throws it at Sister Anne. It says: "Roses are red, violets are blue, don't let Sister Anne get any black on you." We talked about what this rhyme might mean. Nobody answered immediately. Most of the children disagreed with the idea that our skin color can wipe off, but after a few minutes Ellie brought the conversation back to touching and turning skin black. We discussed how the parents in the book were misguidedly afraid for their children to be in Sister Anne's classroom. Some students continued to bring up the rhyme and wondered if skin color could indeed transfer; the rhyme had literal meaning for them. I asked an African American boy to touch another student and then I asked the students what happened.

My decision to have a Black student "wipe" his skin on a White student's is problematic. Why did I not ask it the other way around (White

FIGURE 8.3. Logan's Painting

student to wipe skin on a Black student)? More than that, it is troubling how this interaction reinforces the idea of race as skin color (biological). It is also disturbing that I positioned a boy who is African American, in front of all his peers, to touch another child. Perhaps this boy was struggling with his own identities as an African American child (or maybe he was not), but it was not my place (as a teacher with authority) to ask (really tell) him to wipe his skin on someone else. Did my interaction posit the African American child as the Other and the Caucasian as the norm (as opposed to White being able to wipe off)? I still wonder how my request and his action made the boy feel.

Later that day, I heard a few children rereading the book, focusing specifically on the rhyme, and still trying to understand if our skin color can really "wipe off" on another person's skin, using their bodies to test out their hypotheses.

This example illustrates how young children used their bodies and imaginations in relation to one another. Their play was a way of understanding an issue they were wrestling with related to segregation. We used images in the book to help us process the injustices of racism and segregation, but conversation did not stay there. The students' embodied social action by trying to prove to one another that skin tone does not "wipe off." Through role-play, in relationship to one another, they were co-constructing meaning in how their peers understand race, which in turn appeared to help them understand the unjustified accusations in the paper airplane letter.

Experiences through role-play assisted them to understand that race is not about skin color, but socially constructed ideas related to fear and power.

MOMENTS OF CONSCIOUSNESS-RAISING

While I acknowledge that tangible, larger-scale social action through various types of projects is powerful and an effective part of critical literacy inquiries, based on my experiences I wonder if these are the only ways to achieve social action. We can reconsider what counts as social action. I believe that a lot of change took place not only during the summer program but possibly even after our time together. As Sahni (2001) writes, social action takes place in the imagined possibilities of students' writing and new ways of relating to others. As Lewis et al. (2007) posit, social action "is about kids performing their identities moment-to-moment, shifting and destabilizing classroom power relations . . . social action is performative" (p. 7). Social action does not always have to be visible in a large-scale, planned project, such as in a class petition or a survey. As people, we live out our feelings and learning in such a way that they have potential to influence future interactions and beliefs. This is action; it is a powerful and valid aspect of critical literacy.

Of course, I also have to take a critical eye toward what happened related to the playground incident. Is stating social action as embodied a way of defending or justifying that we did not participate in a large-scale project such as writing a letter to Mrs. Adams or approaching her with our requests for sharing the bench? Some people might read the situation as such. Was it my fault as the teacher that we did not approach Mrs. Adams? Was I, too, afraid of interacting with her about the bench? Was I afraid of how she might respond and the ways that might compromise the students' relationship with her or me? Maybe the answer is yes to these questions, even though that is difficult to admit. Power does circulate in relationships at schools both for children and adults. I was reluctant to approach Mrs. Adams as discussed in Chapter 4. I do not think there was an official summer program rule about adults and children sitting on playground benches, however, it was an expected way of being on the playground for Mrs. Adams. Perhaps this was an official rule at the school she worked at during the regular school year. As discussed previously, I also felt uncomfortable and powerless, as I did not have a prior relationship with Mrs. Adams and was younger than her. I too, perhaps like the students, felt conflicted about speaking up to someone older than me. Would it be perceived as disrespectful? Would it compromise our working relationship? Speaking up was a risk, at the time, I was not willing to take.

As a child, the experiences I had with family, at church, at school, and with friends shaped how I view acts in the world as just or not. Even decades later, these experiences—such as the classrooms in my school basement and church vacation Bible school experiences with traditionally marginalized groups—have all stuck with me. As Webster and Mertova (2007) write, these are critical narrative events. Many times we do not know the impact these stories have on us in the moment; it is not until later that we are able to identify these crucial stories in our life narratives. We all have critical narrative events. These moments, even over time and space, can provoke social change on a personal and a larger scale. Childhood and my beginning teaching experiences still shape me today. Events are sedimented in and form our identities over time and space—influenced by different communities, cultures, relationships, schooling experiences, religions, and so forth. (Rowsell & Pahl, 2007). How we choose to respond to our experiences whether in daily interactions with friends, loved ones, or strangers can all be forms of social action. Social action can happen in day-to-day occurrences and relationships as well as large-scale group endeavors.

Teaching and reflecting helped stretch my beliefs and unlearn my previous ideas of what social action is. As educators, we need to acknowledge and provide spaces in curriculum for children to wrestle with social injustices that they experience and/or witness. Daily interactions can be critical moments of consciousness-raising for children (and adults).

CHAPTER 9

Tensions as Productive Resources

Consciousness-Raising
as an Ongoing Process

Hillary Janks argues that tensions are productive for critical literacy teaching and learning (Pahl & Rowsell, 2012). Tensions are resources, and therefore, even though teaching from a critical stance can be hard at times and is infused with consistent reflexivity, the tensions can be productive. As a concluding chapter, I discuss how the tensions of teaching from a critical literacy stance coupled with autoethnographic processes are difficult but necessary for living and teaching critically.

I discuss moments of uncertainty, focusing on instances where I found myself having an inner dialogue about what to do or say next, unsure where to go in conversations with the students. Then I share struggles in living out critical literacy in teaching and ways I found to embrace the tensions as resources. I use examples from my audio reflection journals, which illuminate the tensions of reflecting, and how talking into an audio recorder every afternoon on the way home served as a space of reflexivity. Finally, I encourage educators to consider life as an autoethnographic process. Autoethnography is not a one-time event but a way of living and teaching that evolves over time in relationships with others. Consciousness-raising is an ongoing, changing process.

MOMENTS OF UNCERTAINTY

Moments of uncertainty in teaching are productive, as they nudge curricular spaces for reflection, dialogue, and social action. As previously stated, I deliberately chose not to give Annie (and the other students) up front my answer as to why segregation laws were created. I wanted students to have time and space to research and deliberate about this injustice. I did not want my teaching to come across as dogmatic. This was a conscious decision I made, in part because I did not have a long history with these children and their families. I truly wanted to approach the curriculum from an inquiry standpoint, not with me as the knowledge-giver to the students' questions. I also wanted to give the students the opportunity to make their own decisions.

However, by choosing not to give Annie direct answers to her questions about segregation, I believe my position shifted in relation to her. Instead of seeing me as a person to give her answers, as teachers are so often viewed, she conceivably saw me as someone co-constructing understanding about segregation. For example, when Annie asked me who the "poor one" was at the water fountain, photographed in the picture book we were looking at together, I responded that I was not sure. This again illustrates how difficult it can be for a teacher to have conversations about topics of injustice with children and try to remain somewhat impartial at first so they have space and time to explore their own feelings before being influenced by the teacher. At the same time, I wanted to be honest with the students and share my perspectives. Leaving room for uncertainty in curriculum is risky and can feel tenuous. However, it provides space to follow students' questions and allows space for critical dialogue and possible social action.

When talking one-on-one with another student, Logan, I discussed how hard the playground incident was for me (Kuby, 2013c), I told him I was not sure how to respond to Mrs. Adams, noting that the requests by her made me feel really uncomfortable. Logan appeared to struggle with discussing this topic. He stated, "OK this is hard." I agreed with Logan about how hard the conversation was between the two of us to discuss the playground incident. When I told him I disagreed with another teacher, he did not hesitate at all to tell me how I should have responded to Mrs. Adams. Logan said, "I think [you should] talk to her." With exasperation in his voice, he told me that he could not "even handle grown-ups." This conversation was a risk for me: talking with Logan and the class about how I disagreed with another teacher, I knew there was a chance that word might get around in such a way that Mrs. Adams could be angry at my decisions.

With Annie, my choice to open up about how I disagreed with bus segregation was a little more removed from my personal life, as laws today allow for people to sit where they want on a bus. However, with Logan and the playground scenario, I was very much a character. I was intimately involved by witnessing and experiencing the bench incident and by choosing to bring these observations back to the class for discussion. By choosing to open curricular space for students to talk, I was risking my position among other teachers. Logan was taking a risk as well, finally opening up to me about his perspective.

Moments of uncertainty in teaching are productive. When Annie asked questions I was not expecting or Logan finally opened up about his experience on the bench, I was unsure what to do. But through intentionally reflecting, actively listening to their words, and observing their body language, I opened curricular spaces for the students to critically dialogue.

LIVING OUT CRITICAL LITERACY IN TEACHING

As Vasquez (2004) writes, critical literacy is lived. This means that the daily interactions in a classroom should embody the tenets of critical literacy. This was difficult. Daily audio reflections illuminate how difficult it was each day to live out teaching from a critical stance, to decide what to teach and how to structure class time, as well as to engage in a constant state of reflexivity as a teacher researcher. Below are two audio reflection journal entries from the last week of the summer program that highlight how difficult it was for me as a teacher researcher to live out critical, socially just practices in a school environment where I did not have a relationship with other teachers.

> Today on the playground, I was walking out to the bench. Logan was sitting there [with a friend]. Mrs. Adams started yelling at them as she was walking out. I was a few steps behind her and felt really uncomfortable. I wanted to see their response but at the same time I didn't want to sit down. I just wasn't sure what to do. Logan kind of gave this grimace or this look like he was sad but he got up anyway. I'd like to talk with him one-on-one and see what his thoughts are. (Teaching Reflection Notes, Monday, July 7)

The above entry highlights that even after 6 weeks with the students to build relationships, teaching from a critical stance was still not easy. I contemplated, should I sit on the bench or not? Should I say something to Mrs. Adams? What did my embodied actions say to my students? The next day I reflected on a conversation I had with Logan one-on-one on the playground. The following reflective memo captures the tensions I felt.

> It's a really tough situation for him [Logan] or for kids in general, I'm noticing, because he feels like he should be able to sit on the bench. But [he does] not [want] to be disrespectful to adults. How do I help children find their voice, how to say things, and have conversations with adults in a way that lets them express what they're feeling and what they think? [I don't want them to] be socialized by rules [that state] adults get the bench [and] kids don't. [This is] really difficult, really tough. I had to admit to him that I wasn't sure what to say or do.

I made a connection to the book called *Say Something* (Moss, 2008), where the main character was hoping that the other friends at her lunch table would say something to help her. But they sat, were quiet, and that upset her. It kind of made me feel a little guilty that I wasn't sure what to say to this teacher when I noticed that Logan was not able to sit in the shade. So it's [critical literacy] difficult, difficult for me too. (Teaching Reflection Notes, Tuesday, July 8)

Living out critical literacy was not easy, even though I hold many deep personal beliefs about inequities and the need for critical dialogue and action. It was not enough to believe in the injustice of segregation and that children should have a voice in playground rules. I had to find ways to create curricular spaces for the children and I to dialogue about inequities. I discovered that when teaching children from a critical perspective, one needs other educators to lean on, to go to with questions, and to share similar beliefs on living and teaching. I turned periodically to a graduate school colleague, not affiliated with the summer program, who lives out critical literacy to share my thoughts and ask for advice on planning.

MAKING SENSE OF TENSIONS AS RESOURCES

It is a myth that teaching is neutral. I do not believe one can choose to never utter an ideological statement, because choosing to avoid certain topics makes a statement in and of itself about one's beliefs. I resonate with Maria Sweeney (1999), who writes, "I don't pretend that my teaching is neutral or objective; education never is. Behind everything taught is a point of view or particular perspective. Value-free education is a myth and, in fact, an impossibility" (p. 97).

A criticism of critical literacy is that it can be or is dogmatic, wherein a teacher imposes his or her beliefs on students about social justice issues. The ebb and flow of my conversations with the students—for example, with Annie and Logan—supports the notion that critical conversations with children do not have to be dogmatic in nature. Instead, it can be dialogical: both people are learning and co-constructing as they go. By reading my students' expressions, listening to their questions, and observing their interactions, I was better able to co-create learning experiences together. The idea of a negotiated curriculum can feel very uncertain to a teacher, especially when teachers are typically taught to write out pre-planned lessons. The Latin etymology of "curriculum" means "running a course or path." This is fitting for teaching, as we do not know what course or path the students' inquiries will take us on; we have to be flexible in our planning to follow the interests of students. For example, I observed the incident on the playground and chose to use this as part of the official curriculum. However, each day students had new questions and suggestions which influenced curriculum planning. I also chose when and how to share my beliefs with my students. However, I question how much choice students really had in sharing their beliefs. For example, they did not actually have a choice to participate in the *Voices on the Bus* learning engagement, though some children did choose to play it safe in their paintings, others seemed to be intentional in the choices they made for the illustrations—intentionally sharing their emotions and thoughts related to bus segregation.

Critical literacy is a curriculum of uncertainty and therefore tensions are expected (Kuby, 2010, 2011a, 2011b). This type of curriculum is a critical social practice where teachers and students co-construct understanding together. Through critical literacy interactions, we are enacting social practices together, therefore as educators we need to view tensions as spaces for growth and change.

LIFE AS AUTOETHNOGRAPHY

Although I was the teacher, I learned so much alongside my students. I learned about the difficulty of co-creating and negotiating a critical inquiry curriculum. I learned that one needs support from others to live out and teach from a critical stance. But on a deeper level I learned about myself. Even though I had conducted an autoethnography before teaching, I now see how life is a constant state of autoethnography if we allow ourselves to live reflexively. Our interactions with people and texts shape our beliefs, and we live life as embodied social action.

In contrast with some developmental views, I am hesitant to say that young children are not aware of injustices and inequities. Children do notice and experience injustices in their lives. I do not see the role of a teacher as being to simply raise awareness, but instead to foster spaces for critical conversations, encourage learning engagements that allow children to wrestle with injustices, and provide opportunities for response and action. If children do not have spaces to talk about critical issues in the world around them, then dominant practices have the potential to become normalized. In early childhood classrooms, it is important to create spaces within the curriculum to explore social issues—this too has potential to be an autoethnographic space and process for young children.

As indicated in one of my last journal entries, the tensions and reflection as a teacher proved fruitful in my growth. Even though, in the moment, teaching/researching was very hard, reflecting upon my decisions and interactions helped to clarify my beliefs and pushed me to wrestle more with creating critical literacy inquiry spaces for early childhood children.

> One thing I've realized this summer is it's hard when you get on a topic like this. How do you know how far to go, how far to take it, and how do you know when it's been exhausted? And [when to] switch to something else? I think it's a very fine line of listening to the kids and trying to figure out where are they [and] what other direction can you push them to think about something they might not have been exposed to yet. How do you know when it's too much for them? (Teaching Reflection Notes, Thursday, July 10)

Teaching from points of uncertainty is a constant state of reflections and tensions. These ambiguities are productive. I do not believe one can ever know exactly how to teach from a critical perspective; there is no script for this type of work. It comes from relationships, embedded in a particular context in space and time, in an attempt to truly know someone else and their experiences. Deborah Hicks (2002) writes:

> Part of what defines a teaching relationship is that teachers can be moved to action by the particulars of context—of what they see in others, with others. . . . What is required for critical literacy teaching is not just the right kinds of discourses, but the right kinds of relationships . . . this requires a certain patience, an attendance. Perhaps it requires watching, living with, and reflecting over time. Teachers need support for this kind of work, but rarely do they find it. But what if critical literacy education . . . requires the slowness of historical time, and the complexity and richness of attachments. (pp. 151–152)

Critical dialogue, thinking, social action, and living do take time and materialize in the complexity of relationships.

> "Sometimes we don't see or notice things happening in our lives until we look back after the fact." (Kuby, 2010, p. 33)

Parent Questionnaire

Parent(s) name (optional): _____
Child's name (optional): _____

The purpose of the questionnaire is to help me to get to know your child better, in regards to community and family life outside of the summer program environment. Your name will not be used in future research, presentations and/or papers. While I would appreciate feedback on all questions, it is not required.

1. Describe the places your family visits on a regular basis (local places as well as outside your local community).

2. Describe the people that your child interacts with regularly.

3. Describe your child's schooling experiences (during the regular school year—not this summer program) in regards to the following areas:

   a. Describe the building and grounds of your child's school.

   b. Describe your child's school's resources.

   c. What activities does your child like to participate in outside of the regular classroom (i.e., extracurricular school or community activities)?

   d. Describe your child's school's learning atmosphere.

4. Please respond to the questions in the table below.

	Do you have conversations with your child about these topics? (circle either yes or no)	If yes, describe the general content of the conversations.	Who typically initiates these conversations? What sparks these conversations?
People of different ethnicities and/or races	Yes or No		
Homeless people	Yes or No		
Gender issues (i.e., what girls or boys are "allowed/not allowed to do")	Yes or No		
Issues related to fairness	Yes or No		
People that have less economically than your family	Yes or No		

5. Choose the income range that best describes your family:

___ $0–50,000   ___ $151,000–175,000
___ $51,000–100,000   ___ $176,000–200,000
___ $101,000–150,000   ___ $201,000 and above

6. Which category best describes your child (choose all the apply):

__ Caucasian   __ African American   __ Native American

__ Hispanic   __ Asian   __ Other _____

7. Circle one: is your child:

                male   or   female

8. Any additional information you wish to share:

Example of Summer Program Newsletter

News from the Sixes' Class: Week of July 7–11, 2008

Parent(s),

I have really enjoyed learning alongside your child this summer. I hope your family has a great few weeks before school starts back up. Take some trips to the library, play some board games together, enjoy a picnic at a park, visit a museum, or whatever else you might find fun together!

Thank you to those who returned the consent forms for my research. I am looking forward to watching the videotapes from the summer and learning from them during my graduate courses this fall. I appreciate your support with that.

Happy Reading!

Candace ☺

Monday: Today we began by reading, *This is the Dream*, a great book with amazing illustrations about non-violent ways to handle conflict and unfair situations. We learned how to play Checkers—a strategy game to add to our list of math games. This week we are going to music class. After snack and recess, we selected the parts we want to play for our *Mrs. Wishy Washy* performance on Wednesday. We also selected which *City Storm* noise we'll perform. During writing time, we began selecting one book that we want to share with parents on Wednesday. Each child is choosing one book that they believe is an example of their best writing this summer. We are making covers for our books and preparing them to share. Several authors in our class taught us from their writing today such as: patterns with words, editing for missing letter sounds, and revising titles. After several friends shared their Daily News, we focused on the following spelling patterns: "y" that makes the long "e" sound, er, ch, x, and apostrophe "s." We ended our day reading with teachers and making choices for reading centers.

Tuesday: Today we began by reading the book, *Say Something*, looking at how unfair things still happen today—even at schools. This book is helping us to learn how to respond to unfair situations that happen to us. Before playing math games, we had a Number Talk with the following problems: 8+8; 8+1+8+1; and 8+2+8+2. After math games we went to music, snack, and recess. When we returned to the room, we practiced role-playing the two big books, *Mrs. Wishy Washy* and *City Storm* that we'll perform for parents tomorrow at our Learning Celebration. After writing our own books, we got in small groups to practice reading our books that we'll share tomorrow. To end our day, some friends worked on their books and instruments for the celebration tomorrow. Other friends read with teachers and made reading center choices.

Wednesday: This morning we revisited our book, *Say Something*, and discussed things that happened in the book that were unfair and thought about why these situations happened. We also began thinking of things that happen to us which are unfair. We learned a new math game, Sneaky Snake, which involves addition and subtraction. Our Number Talk today was: 3+3+3; 3+3+3+1; and 3+3+3+2. After music, snack, and recess, we return to our room to write our Daily News together and write our own books before our parents came for the celebration. We ended our day by reading and performing: *Mrs. Wishy Washy* and *City Storm*. Then we got in small groups to share one of the books we've authored. After sharing books, we taught our parents some of the math games we've been playing this summer.

Thursday: Today we continued to brainstorm unfair situations in our lives. We wrote words and painted images to show these situations. While doing this we are focusing on what actions we could take in unfair situations to help others in nonviolent ways. Our Number Talk today was: 2+2+2; 2+2+2+1; and 2+2+2+2. The children chose partners to play math games with before going to music. After snack and recess we reread some of our favorite big books and songs from this summer. We continued to write our own books before writing Daily News together. During this time, we focused on various spelling patterns and sight words. To end our day, we read with the teachers and chose different reading centers to learn at before packing up for the day.

Friday: Wow! The last day of the program! We began our morning by finishing our paintings on unfair situations and continued to discuss ways to handle unfair situations in our lives. We had our last Number Talk today: 4+4+4; 4+4+4+1; and 4+4+4+2. We had the chance to choose from all the math games we've learned this summer one last time before going to music. After snack and recess, we reread our favorite big books and songs from this summer. We had a little time to write Daily News and our own books, before joining all the other children in the summer program for an ending assembly. During this celebration, our class performed the big books *Mrs. Wishy Washy* and *City Storm* for the other students at the summer program.

Resources in Literature

A variety of readings on consciousness-raising, specifically of teachers telling their stories, is accessible for educators to use in reflecting on their lives.

Consciousness-Raising and Reflective Practice in Early Childhood Education

Hall, E. L., & Rudkin, J. K. (2011). *Seen and heard: Children's rights in early childhood education.* New York: Teachers College Press.

Jacobson, T. (2003). *Confronting our discomfort: Clearing the way for anti-bias in early childhood.* Portsmouth, NH: Heinemann.

Kuby, C. R. (2013). Personal histories and pedagogical decisions: Using autoethnographic methods to unpack ideologies and experiences. *Teaching & Learning: The Journal of Natural Inquiry and Reflective Practice, 27*(1) 3–18.

Paley, V. G. (2000). *White teacher* (2nd ed.). Cambridge, MA: Harvard University Press.

Wilson, C. (2000). *Telling a different story: Teaching and literacy in an urban preschool.* New York: Teachers College Press.

Teacher Identity and Reflective Practice

Bolton, G. (2001/2010). *Reflective practice: Writing and professional development.* Los Angeles: Sage.

Cahnmann-Taylor, M., & Souto-Manning, M. (2010). *Teachers act up!: Creating multicultural learning communities through theatre.* New York: Teachers College Press.

Derman-Sparks, L., & Ramsey, P. G. (2011). *What if all the kids are White? Antibias multicultural education with young children and families* (2nd ed.). New York: Teachers College Press.

Hoffman-Kipp, P. (2008, Summer). Actualizing democracy: The praxis of teacher identity construction. *Teacher Education Quarterly, 35*(3), 151–164.

Hoffman-Kipp, P., Artiles, A. J., & Lopez-Torres, L. (2003). Beyond reflection: Teacher learning as praxis. *Theory into Practice,42*(3), 248–254.

Hoffman-Kipp, P., & Olsen, B. (2007). Accessing praxis: Practicing theory, theorizing practice in social justice teachers' first year of teaching. In P. Finn & M. Finn

(Eds.), *Teacher education with an attitude* (pp. 141–156). Albany, NY: State University of New York Press.

Howard, G. R. (1999). *We can't teach what we don't know: White teachers, multiracial schools.* New York: Teachers College Press.

Kendall, F. E. (1996). *Diversity in the classroom.* New York: Teachers College Press.

McDermott, M. (2002, Fall). Collaging preservice teacher identity. *Teacher Education Quarterly, 29*(4), 53–68.

Souto-Manning, M. (2010). *Freire, teaching, and learning: Culture circles across contexts.* New York: Peter Lang.

Teaching and Living Out Critical Literacy

Janks, H., Dixon, K., Ferreira, A., Granville, S., & Newfield, D. (2013). *Doing critical literacy: Texts and activities for students and teachers.* New York: Routledge.

Lewison, M., Leland, C., & Harste, J. C. (2008). *Creating critical classrooms: K–8 reading and writing with an edge.* New York: Routledge.

Vasquez, V. M., Tate, S. L., & Harste, J. C. (2013). *Negotiating critical literacies with teachers: Theoretical foundations and pedagogical resources for preservice and inservice contexts.* New York: Routledge.

Whiteness Theory and Perspectives

Fine, M., Weis, L., Powell, L. C., & Wong, L. M. (Eds.). (1997). *Off White: Readings on race, power, and society.* New York: Routledge.

Giroux, H. (1997). Racial politics and the pedagogy of Whiteness. In M. Hill (Ed.), *Whiteness: A critical reader* (pp. 294–315). New York: NYU Press.

Kincheloe, J., Steinberg, S. R., Rodriguez, N. M., & Chennault, R. E. (Eds.). (1998). *White reign: Deploying Whiteness in America.* New York: St. Martin's Griffin.

McIntyre, A. (1997). Making my Whiteness public. In A. McIntyre (Ed.), *Making meaning of Whiteness: Exploring the racial identity of White teachers* (pp. 29–44). Albany, NY: State University of New York Press.

McIntyre, A. (1997). Constructions of Whiteness. In A. McIntyre (Ed.), *Making meaning of Whiteness: Exploring the racial identity of White teachers* (pp. 79–116). Albany, NY: State University of New York Press.

McLaren, P., & Muñoz, J. (2000). Contesting Whiteness: Critical perspectives on the struggle for social justice. In C. J. Ovando & P. McLaren (Eds.), *The politics of multiculturalism and bilingual education: Students and teachers caught in the cross fire* (pp. 23–49). New York: McGraw-Hill.

Mullen, C. A. (1999). Whiteness, cracks, and ink stains: Making cultural identity with Euroamerican preservice teachers. In C. T. P. Diamond & C. A. Mullen (Eds.), *The postmodern educator: Arts-based inquiries and teacher development* (pp. 147–185). New York: Peter Lang.

Tatum, B. (1999). The development of White identity: "I'm not ethnic, I'm just normal." In B. Tatum (Ed.), *Why are all the Black kids sitting together in the cafeteria? And other conversations about race* (pp. 93–113). New York: Basic Books.

Reflective Exercises for Educators

Drawing upon the notion of multimodal literacies (The New London Group, 1996), I attempt to create experiences for students that bring in visual literacy, technology, performances, and writing. While reading or creating art is in and of itself powerful, dialoging with others is also revelatory. Below are resources and learning engagements that I have used with preservice teachers and graduate students. While most are appropriate to use with adults (e.g., preservice teachers, current teachers, and college faculty), some can be adapted to use with children. While the learning engagements themselves are important, it is critical to spend time deconstructing and dialoguing about the videos, artifacts, and activities. Time is needed to process the experiences and reconstruct new, just ways of living. If space for dialogue and social action is not included, students (especially those of privilege) can be left with guilt and reluctant to see how their identities and experiences can create positive social change.

Videos

1. American Anthropological Association. (2008). *Race.* Educational dual disc set. (This is the video mentioned in the Preface that I viewed at the Missouri History Museum).
2. *The Danger of a Single Story* by Chimamanda Adichie (TED talk)—available online. Adichie shares vignettes from her life and encourages people to not view Others as a single story—all people have complex identities and lives.

Learning Engagements

1. Privilege Walks or Who's Here exercises (questions that ask students to move forward/backward or in/out of a circle based on their experiences and identities; examples available online).
2. Artistic responses to personal narratives and readings. For example, provide art supplies (e.g., paints, collage materials, various colors and types of writing utensils, and a variety of paper choices) for students to respond with after reading or watching texts about identities and life experiences. Have students share their artistic responses in groups.
3. "Where I'm From"—George Ella Lyon, poet, shares her poem "Where I'm From" on her website. Guide students through "memory mapping," a pre-writing activity to use their senses and memories to sketch important places and events from their lives. Students create their own poems.

Through conversations question experiences and identities that either marginalize or signify privilege.

4. *The Important Book* by Margaret Wise Brown—read and have students create their own page for a class-wide book using the text and illustration pattern of Brown's book.

5. Create reader's theater scripts from texts (articles, books) and/or from life experiences. Use performance as a way to take on multiple viewpoints and to deconstruct and reconstruct events.

6. Inner dialogues—collect multiple artifacts and photographs from one's life history to explore ideologies, traditions, memories, and relationships. Use the analysis of the artifacts to create an inner dialogue that demonstrates inner thoughts, tensions, and questions. Try multiple genres and/or modes of representing the dialogue (e.g., multivoiced poetry, art, short story, performance, etc.).

Self-Interviews

In my autoethnographic process, I used questions to initiate a self-interview, writing and talking into a recorder to capture responses. The questions prompted me to unpack conversations and memories from my childhood and young adult years. Educators can do this on their own or partner up for small-group interviews.

Questions for Self-Interview

1. Did you notice any injustices in your schooling experience as a young child? As a youth? As a young adult?

2. Did your family talk about injustices in society related to class, race, and gender? If so, describe some of these memories.

3. Describe pivotal moments in your childhood that relate to your beliefs about injustices.

4. How do you perceive your religious affiliation as a child contributing to your beliefs?

5. How did friends shape your beliefs?

6. Describe your community/town growing up. How do you perceive this as a contributing factor to your identities and beliefs?

7. How do you perceive your views about social injustices today? Have they changed since you were a child? If so, why do you think this change has occurred? What contributes to the change?

8. Describe how your social justice stance influences your teaching.

Relationships for Self-Reflection

Intentionally forming relationships with people you might not typically interact with is another way to bring biases and ideologies to consciousness. Some examples include:

1. Intentionally interacting with people of different races and ethnicities. Examples from my life include: attending Martin Luther King Jr. vigils and

remembrance marches; attending a posthumous funeral in my community for an African American man lynched for an alleged rape of a young girl; and attending fund-raisers for local nonprofit groups that support immigrants in the community.

2. Intentionally interacting with people who are homeless. Examples from my life include: volunteering to work overnight shifts in a low-barrier winter shelter; listening to people who are homeless tell their life stories.

3. Intentionally interacting with people in the LGTBQ community. Examples from my life include: attending pride events to stand as an ally; attending a church that is officially opening/affirming/welcoming to the LGTBQ community.

4. Intentionally interacting with people of different religious beliefs. Examples from my life include: attending services and worship events of other faith traditions than my own, not in an attempt to change them but in order to experience and accept other ways of being spiritual; living abroad in a country that is not predominately Christian.

5. Intentionally interacting with people of different professional foci. Examples from my life include: participating in a writing group with people of different educational fields; attending interdisciplinary conferences.

The examples listed above are some ways and resources that helped me to become more conscious of my biases and ideologies. These examples are just a sampling of ways to provide educators with encounters that might prompt them to consider moments of consciousness-raising in their lives, in hopes of shaping how they teach and research alongside children.

References

Children's Book References

Adler, D. (1995). *A picture book of Rosa Parks*. New York: Holiday House.

Browne, A. (2001). *Voices in the park*. New York: DK Children.

Levine, E. (2007). *Henry's freedom box*. New York: Scholastic Press.

Lorbiecki, M. (2000). *Sister Anne's hands*. New York: Puffin.

Miller, M., & Christie, G. (1999). *Richard Wright and the library card*. New York: Lee & Low Books.

Moss, P. (2008). *Say something*. Gardiner, ME: Tilbury House Publishers.

Schaefer, L. (2000). *Rosa Parks* (First Biographies). North Mankato, MN: Capstone Press.

Shore, D. Z., & Ransome, J. (2005). *This is the dream*. New York: Amistad.

Williams, S. (1992). *I went walking*. New York: Sandpiper.

Woodson, J. (2001). *The other side*. New York: Putnam Juvenile.

Scholarly References

American Anthropological Association. (2008). *Race*. Educational dual disc set.

Albers, P. (1999). Art education and the possibility of social change. *Art Education, 52*(4), 6–11.

Alvermann, D. E. (2000). Researching libraries, literacies, and lives: A rhizoanalysis. In E. A. St. Pierre & W. S. Pillows (Eds.), *Working the ruins: Feminist poststructural theory and methods in education* (pp. 114–129). New York: Routledge.

Atkinson, P., & Delamont, S. (2006). Rescuing narrative from qualitative research. *Narrative Inquiry, 16*(1), 164–172.

Ballenger, C. (1999). *Teaching other people's children: Literacy and learning in a bilingual classroom*. New York: Teachers College Press.

Barton, D., & Hamilton, M. (2000). Literacy practices. In D. Barton, M. Hamilton, & R. Ivanic (Eds.), *Situated literacies* (pp. 7–15). London: Routledge.

Blackburn, M., & Clark, C. (Eds.). (2007). *Literacy research for political action and social change*. New York: Peter Lang.

Bloome, D., Carter, S. P., Christian, B. M., Otto, S., & Shuart-Faris, N. (2005). *Discourse analysis & the study of classroom language & literacy events: A microethnographic perspective*. Mahwah, NJ: Erlbaum.

Boler, M. (1999). *Feeling power: Emotions and education*. New York: Routledge.

Bolton, G. (2001). *Reflective practice: Writing and professional development* (2nd ed.). London: Paul Chapman Publishing.

Bolton, G. (2010). *Reflective practice: Writing and professional development* (3rd ed.). Thousand Oaks, CA: Sage.

Campano, G. (2007). *Immigrant students and literacy: Reading, writing, and remembering*. New York: Teachers College Press.

Carson, C., & Shepard, K. (Eds.). (2001). *A call to conscience: The landmark speeches of Dr. Martin Luther King, Jr.* New York: Hachette Book Group.

Cazden, C. B. (2001). *Classroom discourse: The language of teaching and learning* (2nd ed.). Portsmouth, NH: Heinemann.

Christensen, L. M. (1999). Critical literacy: Teaching reading, writing, and outrage. In C. Edelsky (Ed.), *Making justice our project: Teachers working toward critical whole language practice* (pp. 209–225). Urbana, IL: National Council of Teachers of English.

Clarke, L. W. (2005). "A stereotype is something you listen to music on": Navigating a critical curriculum. *Language Arts, 83*(2), 147–157.

Cochran-Smith, M., & Lytle, S. (Eds.). (1993). *Inside/outside: Teacher research and knowledge*. New York: Teachers College Press.

Cochran-Smith, M., & Lytle, S. (Eds.). (2009). *Inquiry as stance: Practitioner research for the next generation*. New York: Teachers College Press.

Cole, A. L., & Knowles, J. G. (2001). *Lives in context: The art of life history research*. New York: Rowman & Littlefield.

Comber, B., & Nixon, H. (2008). Spatial literacies, design, texts, and emergent pedagogies in purposeful literacy curriculum. *Pedagogies: An International Journal, 3*(4), 221–240.

Comber, B., Nixon, H., Ashmore, L., Loo, S., & Cook, J. (2006). Urban renewal from the inside out: Spatial and critical literacies in a low socioeconomic school community. *Mind, Culture, and Activity, 13*(3), 228–246.

Comber, B., & Simpson, A. (Eds.). (2001). *Negotiating critical literacies in classrooms*. Mahwah, NJ: Erlbaum.

Cowhey, M. (2006). *Black ants and Buddhists: Thinking critically and teaching differently in the primary grades*. Portland, ME: Stenhouse.

Deleuze, G., & Guattari, F. (1987). *A thousand plateaus: Capitalism and schizophrenia* (B. Massumi, Trans.). Minneapolis: University of Minnesota Press.

Delpit, L. (1995). *Other people's children: Cultural conflict in the classroom*. New York: New Press.

Delpit, L. (2002). *The skin that we speak: Thoughts on language and culture in the classroom*. New York: New Press.

Derman-Sparks, L., & Ramsey, P. (2011). *What if all the kids are White?: Anti-bias multicultural education with young children and families* (2nd ed.). New York: Teachers College Press.

Duncan, M. (2004). Autoethnography: Critical appreciation of an emerging art. *International Journal of Qualitative Methods, 3*(4), 1–14.

Edelsky, C. (Ed.). (1999). *Making justice our project: Teachers working toward critical whole language practice*. Urbana, IL: National Council of Teachers of English.

Ellingson, L. L. (2009). *Engaging in crystallization in qualitative research: An introduction*. Thousand Oaks, CA: Sage.

Ellis, C., & Bochner, A. (2006). Analyzing analytic autoethnography: An autopsy. *Journal of Contemporary Ethnography, 35*(4), 429–449.

Ellsworth, E. (1989). Why doesn't this feel empowering? Working through the repressive myths of critical pedagogy. *Harvard Educational Review, 59*(3), 297–324.

Ellsworth, E. (1992). Why doesn't this feel empowering? Working through the repressive myths of critical pedagogy. In A. Luke & J. Gore (Eds.), *Feminisms and critical pedagogy* (pp. 90–119). New York: Routledge.

Evans, J. (2007). War and peas in the 21st century: Young children responding critically to picture story texts. In Y. M. Goodman & P. Martens (Eds.), *Critical issues in early literacy: Research and pedagogy* (pp. 235–250). Mahwah, NJ: Erlbaum.

Fairclough, N. (1989). *Language and power*. London: Longman.

Fairclough, N. (1992). *Discourse and social change*. Cambridge, MA: Polity Press.

Foucault, M. (1977). *Discipline and punish: The birth of the prison*. New York: Vintage Books.

Fecho, B., & Meacham, S. (2007). Learning to play and playing to learn: Research sites as transactional spaces. In C. Lewis, P. Enciso, & E. B. Moje (Eds.), *Reframing sociocultural research on literacy: Identity, agency, and power* (pp. 163–188). Mahwah, NJ: Erlbaum.

Fine, M. (1997). Witnessing Whiteness. In M. Fine, L. Weis, L. C. Powell, & L. M. Wong (Eds.), *Off white: Readings on race, power, and society* (pp. 57–65). New York: Routledge.

Fine, M., Weis, L., Powell, L. C., & Wong, L. M. (Eds.). (1997). *Off white: Readings on race, power, and society*. New York: Routledge.

Fisher, B. (1998). *Joyful learning in kindergarten* (2nd ed.). Portsmouth, NH: Heinemann.

Freire, P. (2005). *Pedagogy of the oppressed* (30th anniversary ed.). New York: Continuum. (Original work published 1970)

Gannon, S., & Davies, B. (2007). Postmodern, poststructural, and critical theories. In S. N. Hesse-Biber (Eds.), *Handbook of feminist research: Theory and praxis* (pp. 71–106). Thousand Oaks, CA: Sage.

Gee, J. P. (1996). *Social linguistics and literacies: Ideology in discourses* (2nd ed.). New York: Routledge.

Gee, J. P. (2005). *An introduction to discourse analysis: Theory and method* (2nd ed.). New York: Routledge.

Giroux, H. (1997). Racial politics and the pedagogy of Whiteness. In M. Hill (Ed.), *Whiteness: A critical reader* (pp. 294–315). New York: NYU Press.

Glesne, C. (2005). *Becoming a qualitative researcher: An introduction* (3rd ed.). New York: Allyn & Bacon.

Goodson, I. (1998) Storying the self. In W. Pinar (Ed.), *Curriculum: Towards new identities* (pp. 3–20). New York: Taylor & Francis.

Gramsci, A. (1971). *Selections from the prison notebooks*. New York: International Publishers Co.

Gutierrez, K., & Larson, J. (1994). Language borders: Recitation as hegemonic discourse. *International Journal of Educational Reform, 3*(1), 22–36.

Hankins, K. H. (2003). *Teacher through the storm: A journal of hope*. New York: Teachers College Press.

Harste, J., & Vasquez, V. (1998). The work we do: Journal as audit trail. *Language Arts, 75*(4), 266–276.

Hawkesworth, M. (2007). Truth and truths in feminist knowledge production. In S. N. Hesse-Biber (Ed.), *Handbook of feminist research: Theory and praxis* (pp. 469–491). Thousand Oaks, CA: Sage.

Heffernan, L., & Lewison, M. (2000). Making real-world issues our business: Critical literacy in a third-grade classroom. *Primary Voices K-6, 9*(2), 15–21.

Heffernan, L., & Lewison, M. (2003). Social narrative writing: (Re)constructing kids culture in the writer's workshop. *Language Arts, 80*(6), 435–443.

Heffernan, L., & Lewison, M. (2005). What's lunch got to do with it? Critical literacy and the discourse of the lunchroom. *Language Arts, 83*(2), 107–117.

Helm, J. H., & Katz, L. (2011). *Young investigators: The project approach in the early years* (2nd ed.). New York: Teachers College Press.

Hicks, D. (2002). *Reading lives: Working-class children and literacy learning*. New York: Teachers College Press.

hooks, b. (1992). *Black looks: Race and representation*. New York: South End Press.

Humphreys, M. (2005). Getting personal: Reflexivity and autoethnographic vignettes. *Qualitative Inquiry, 11*(6), 840–860.

Jacobson, T. (2003). *Confronting our discomfort: Clearing the way for anti-bias in early childhood*. Portsmouth, NH: Heinemann.

Jones, S. H. (2003). The way we were, are, and might be: Torch singing as autoethnography. In Y. S. Lincoln & N. K. Denzin (Eds.), *Turning points in qualitative research: Tying knots in a handkerchief* (pp. 105–120). New York: Altamira Press.

Jones, S. H. (2005). Autoethnography: Making the personal political. In N. K. Denzin & Y. S. Lincoln (Eds.), *The Sage handbook of qualitative research* (3rd ed., pp. 763–791). Thousand Oaks, CA: Sage.

Jones, S. H. (2007). Autoethnography. In G. Ritzer (Ed.), *Blackwell encyclopedia of sociology*. Malden, MA: Blackwell.

Jones, S. (2006). *Girls, social class, and literacy: What teachers can do to make a difference*. Portsmouth, NH: Heinemann.

Kincheloe, J. L., & McLaren, P. (2005). Rethinking critical theory and qualitative research. In N. Denzin & Y. Lincoln (Eds.), *The Sage handbook of qualitative research* (3rd ed., pp. 303–342). Thousand Oaks, CA: Sage.

Kincheloe, J., Steinberg, S. R., Rodriguez, N. M., & Chennault, R. E. (Eds.). (1998). *White reign: Deploying Whiteness in America*. New York: St. Martin's Griffin.

Kramer-Dahl, A. (1996). Reconsidering the notions of voice and experience in critical pedagogy. In C. Luke (Ed.), *Feminism and pedagogies of everyday life* (pp. 242–262). Albany: State University of New York Press.

Kuby, C. R. (2010). *Understanding an early childhood inquiry curriculum through crystallizing autoethnography, practitioner research, and a performative analysis of emotion* (Doctoral Dissertation, Indiana University). Available from ProQuest Dissertations & Theses database (UMI No. 3413651).

Kuby, C. R. (2011a). Humpty Dumpty and Rosa Parks: Making space for critical dialogue with 5 and 6 year olds. *Young Children, 66*(5), 36–43.

Kuby, C. R. (2011b). Kidwatching with a critical eye: The power of observation and reflexive practice. *Talking Points, 22*(2), 22–28.

Kuby, C. R. (2012). Synaesthetic responses to children's illustrations. In K. Pahl & J. Rowsell (Eds.), *Literacy and education* (pp. 32–33). Thousand Oaks, CA: Sage.

Kuby, C. R. (2013a). Learning from artistic encounters: A teacher's experience with young children's painting of racial bus segregation. In V. Vasquez & J. Wood (Eds.), *Perspectives and provocations in early childhood education* (pp. 69–87). Charlotte, NC: Information Age Publishing.

Kuby, C. R. (2013b). Evoking emotions and unpacking layered histories through young children's illustration of racial bus segregation. *Journal of Early Childhood Literacy, 13*(2), 271–300.

Kuby, C. R. (2013c). "OK this is hard": Doing emotions in social justice dialogue. *Education, Citizenship, and Social Justice, 8*(1), 29–42.

Kuby, C.R. (in press). Crystallization as a methodology: Disrupting traditional ways of analyzing and (re)presenting through multiple genres. In R.N. Brown, R. Carducci, & C.R. Kuby (Eds.), *Disrupting qualitative inquiry: Possibilities and tensions in educational research*. New York: Peter Lang.

Lewis, A. E. (2004). "What group?" Studying Whites and Whiteness in the era of "color-blindness." *Sociological Theory, 22*(4), 623–646.

Lewis, C. (2001). *Literary practices as social acts: Power, status, and cultural norms in the classroom*. Mahwah, NJ: Erlbaum.

Lewis, C., Enciso, P., & Moje, E. B. (Eds.). (2007). *Reframing sociocultural research on literacy*. Mahwah, NJ: Erlbaum.

Lewison, M., Leland, C., & Harste, J. (2007). *Creating critical classrooms*. Mahwah, NJ: Erlbaum.

Lyotard, J. P. (1992). *The postmodern explained to children*. London: Turnaround.

McIntyre, A. (1997). *Making meaning of Whiteness: Exploring the racial identity of White teachers*. Albany, NY: State University of New York Press.

McLaren, P., & Muñoz, J. (2000). Contesting Whiteness: Critical perspectives on the struggle for social justice. In C. J. Ovando & P. McLaren (Eds.), *The politics of multiculturalism and bilingual education: Students and teachers caught in the cross fire* (pp. 23–49). New York: McGraw-Hill.

Mehan, H. (1979). *Learning lessons: Social organization in the classroom*. Cambridge, MA: Harvard University Press.

Morrell, E. (2004). *Becoming critical researchers: Literacy and empowerment for urban youth*. New York: Lang.

Muncey, T. (2005). Doing autoethnography. *International Journal of Qualitative Research, 4*(3), 1–12.

New London Group. (1996). A pedagogy of multiliteracies: Designing social futures. *Harvard Educational Review 66*(1), 60–92.

Pahl, K., & Rowsell, J. (2012). *Literacy and education* (2nd ed.). Thousand Oaks, CA: Sage.

Richardson, L., & St. Pierre, E. A. (2005). Writing: A method of inquiry. In N. K. Denzin & Y. S. Lincoln (Eds.), *The Sage handbook of qualitative research* (3rd ed., pp. 959–978). Thousand Oaks, CA: Sage.

Riessman, C. K. (2008). *Narrative methods for the human sciences.* Los Angeles: Sage.

Rowsell, J., & Pahl, K. (2007). Sedimented identities in texts: Instances of practice. *Reading Research Quarterly, 42*(3), 388–404.

Said, E., (1978). *Orientalism.* New York: Pantheon Books.

Sahni, U. (2001). Children appropriating literacy: Empowerment pedagogy from young children's perspective. In B. Comber & A. Simpson (Eds.), *Negotiating critical literacies in classrooms* (pp. 19–36). Mahwah, NJ: Erlbaum.

Sleeter, C. E. (1993). How White teachers construct race. In C. McCarthy & W. Critchlow (Eds.), *Race, identity, & representation in education* (pp. 157–171). New York: Routledge.

Smith, C. (2005). Epistemological intimacy: A move to autoethnography. *International Journal of Qualitative Methods, 4*(2), 1–12.

Souto-Manning, M. (2009). Negotiating culturally responsive pedagogy through multicultural children's literature: Towards critical democratic literacy practices in a first grade classroom. *Journal of Early Childhood Literacy, 9*(1), 50–74.

Spry, T. (2001). Performing autoethnography: An embodied methodological praxis. *Qualitative Inquiry, 7*(6), 706–732.

Stockett, K. (2009). *The help.* New York: Amy Einhorn Books/Putnam.

Street, B. V. (1984). *Literacy in theory and practice.* New York: Cambridge University Press.

Street, B. V. (2000). Literacy events and literacy practices: Theory and practice in the New Literacy Studies. In M. Martin-Jones (Ed.), *Multilingual matters* (pp. 17–29). Philadelphia: J. Benjamins.

Sweeney, M. (1999). Critical literacy in a fourth-grade classroom. In C. Edelsky (Ed.), *Making justice our project: Teachers working toward critical whole language practice* (pp. 96–114). Urbana, IL: National Council of Teachers of English.

Tatum, B. (1999). The development of White identity: "I'm not ethnic, I'm just normal." In B. Tatum (Ed.), *Why are all the Black kids sitting together in the cafeteria? And other conversations about race* (pp. 93–113). New York: Basic Books.

Van Leeuwen, T., & Jewitt, C. (2001). *Handbook of visual analysis.* London: Sage.

Vasquez, V. M. (2001). Constructing a critical curriculum with young children. In B. Comber & A. Simpson (Eds.), *Negotiating critical literacies in classrooms* (pp. 55–68). Mahwah, NJ: Erlbaum.

Vasquez, V. M. (2004). *Negotiating critical literacies with young children.* Mahwah, NJ: Erlbaum.

Vasquez, V. M. (2005). Creating opportunities for critical literacy with young children: Using everyday issues and everyday texts. In J. Evans (Ed.), *Literacy moves on: Popular culture, new technologies, and critical literacy in the elementary classroom* (pp. 83–105). Portsmouth, NH: Heinemann.

Wall, S. (2006). An autoethnography on learning about autoethnography. *International Journal of Qualitative Methods, 5*(2), 1–12.

Webster, L., & Mertova, P. (2007). *Using narrative inquiry as a research method.* New York: Routledge.

Wink, J. (2000). *Critical pedagogy: Notes from the real world* (2nd ed.). New York: Longman.

Wohlwend, K. (2007). Friendship meeting or blocking circle: Identities in the laminated spaces of a playground conflict. *Contemporary Issues in Early Childhood, 8*(1), 73–88.

Zembylas, M. (2005). Discursive practices, genealogies, and emotional rules: A poststructuralist view on emotion and identity in teaching. *Teaching and Teacher Education, 21*, 935–948.

Index